Chatter of Choughs

Chatter of Choughs

A St. Edmund Hall Anthology
of Poems and Essays

Edited by Lucy Newlyn

with a Foreword by Michael Mingos, FRS

This edition published in 2001 by
Signal Books Ltd.
36 Minster Road
Oxford

in association with St Edmund Hall, Oxford

A catalogue record for this book is available from the British Library.

ISBN 1-902669-50-9 Paper
ISBN 1-902669-51-7 Cloth

Cover design: 'Chough on a moonlit night doing a spectaclar acrobatic
display somewhere over Cornwall in the region of Mousehole' by
Stephen Farthing, R.A.

Illustrations by Lucy Wilkinson, Geoffrey Bourne-Taylor and others

Typesetting by Toby Milner

Printed in the United Kingdom

Contents

PART ONE: The Cornish Chough
Illustrations by Lucy Wilkinson

PART TWO: Prophetic Birds
Illustrations by Lucy Wilkinson

PART THREE: Arthurian Choughs

Illustrations by Lucy Wilkinson

PART FOUR: Chuffed

Illustrations by Geoffrey Bourne-Taylor and others

PART FIVE: Teddy Hall Choughs
Illustrations by Geoffrey Bourne-Taylor and others

PART SIX: Chough Frenzy – In the Workshop

Dedication

To Graham Midgley, Reggie Alton, and Bruce Mitchell

Foreword

by Michael Mingos, FRS, Principal of St Edmund Hall

A recent poll commissioned by Radio 4 suggested that 'serendipity' was the most interesting word in the English language. Serendipity also describes precisely the complex and unpredictable series of events which led to the publication of this delightful book. Last Autumn after a graduation lunch I received on behalf of the Hall a pair of well preserved stuffed Cornish choughs in a glass case. Mr Broughton, the father of Jacqui Broughton who was graduating on that day, had come across the specimens in an antique shop many years before. As a vet he had recognised their rarity and significance, and decided to purchase them. He felt that as his daughter was graduating from a College whose coat of arms included four Cornish choughs it was appropriate to pass them on to the College for safe keeping. I gratefully accepted them at the ceremony and after the appropriate pictures had been taken I placed them temporarily on the mantelpiece of the dining room of the lodgings, recognising that in an Oxford College it might take some discussion and negotiation before a final resting place for the birds could be agreed by the Fellows.

Each year on 16th November the Hall celebrates St. Edmund by holding a formal dinner to which third year undergraduates, Fellows and guests of the Fellows are inivited. It is a tradition – or so I was told when I took up the Principalship in 1999 – for the Principal to give an after dinner speech on such occasions. Since I am neither a natural nor a gifted public speaker such an event does prey on my mind until I find some theme which provides a scaffold for the speech, or at least provokes some gallows-humour. The previous year I had spoken about the life of St Edmund and was anxiously seeking another topic. In our dining hall we have three large banners which are based on the College Coat of Arms and our association with St Edmund and Osney Abbey. I chose to use these as a basis for my speech. Since I knew nothing about the choughs which adorned our coat of arms I thought that I ought to do some preliminary research and so typed "chough" into my computer . This created a long list of cricket clubs, but not much useful information except the species name "Pyrrhocorax " which was re-submitted into the search engine. The web-sites which resulted revealed all that I needed for my talk and included pictures of choughs, their distribution across the

Northern Hemisphere and even a poem by Dorothy Williams entitled "The White-Winged Chough" which gave a humorous twist to the bizarre and alternative pronounciations of the -ough ending in the English language. This I thought would give a suitable end to the speech and provide some mild amusement to the foreign students who were attending the dinner.

I also thought that since I was speaking about Cornish choughs and few of the guests would have seen one in real life it might be instructive to place the stuffed specimens in front of me once the meal was complete and the tables had been relaid for dessert and speeches. (Their presence at an earlier stage of the meal might have been off-putting.) I had a further ulterior motive – I knew that Terry Jones who was one of the Monty Python group was going to be at the dinner as an Honorary Fellow of the College and it would give me the opportunity of making a useful allusion to the classic 'dead parrot' joke. Well, all went reasonably to plan and I felt I could forget for another ten months the topic of my St Edmund speech.

A couple of days later I received from Lucy Newlyn a letter suggesting that it might be a good idea to assemble a book of poems inspired by choughs. I was not wildly enthusiastic, but encouraged her to explore the matter further. I underestimated her tenacity and the ability of choughs to evoke a positive response from poets and colleagues. So although I can recognise how the project originated from a moment of desperation in my mind I do not recognise or understand the cascade of events which followed and led to this extensive and beautifully illustrated book of poems and essays.

As a scientist I would define a catalyst as something which accelerates a chemical reaction, but remains unchanged as a result of the process. I can recognise my role as an unconscious catalyst for what happened, but I cannot admit to being unchanged by the process. I have been humbled and moved to see how "choughs" have managed to unlock the imaginations of recognised poets, but also to release the talents of amateur poets to produce a volume which is at once amusing, thought-provoking and evocative. It is also a reminder for scientists such as myself that human behaviour can be influenced disproportionately by a few well chosen words and phrases. Clearly, the word "chough" creates waves in the human mind which evoke memories and symbols stretching from the childhood idealism of King Arthur and the Round Table, through Shakespeare's symbol of prophecy, to modern environmental concerns. Therefore, "chough" like serendipity evokes a widespread reaction and I am sure that all who read this volume will find something which refreshes their minds and touches their emotions.

Michael Mingos
St. Edmund Hall, April 2001

photograph by Stacey Mingos

Acknowledgements

Many thanks to all the contributors to this anthology for entering so readily into its spirit, making it such an enjoyable collaboration. I am particularly grateful to the Principal, the Bursar, Rachel Cable, Emma Steane, and Felicity Hampson for all the help they have given in getting the book together.

The anthology could not have been published without financial sponsorship from the SEH Association and the following donors: Michael Cansdale, David Dunsmore, David Graham, Derek Hockridge, John Lloyd, David Short, Frank Spooner, Robert Strapps, George Wiley, Douglas Wilson, and John Young. A special thank you to Michael Cansdale for his fund-raising zest and tenacity, as well as his enthusiastic support of the enterprise from its first inception. Thanks also to Arthur Farrand Radley, who has generously shared his knowledge of choughs, accumulated over many years.

Most of the poems have been specially written for the volume; but we are grateful for permission to reprint the following: 'Chough' from Rex Warner's *Poems and Contradictions* (John Lane, 1945); 'Back' from Jem Poster's *Brought to Light* (Bloodaxe, 2001); 'Chough' from Andrew McNellie's *Nevermore* (Cacrcanet, 2000); 'Choughs' from Gillian Clarke's *Collected Poems* (Carcanet, 1997); and Dorothy Williams's 'The White Winged Chough' from Woorilla Poetry.

Preface

Teddy Hall is a chough college. You see them everywhere, as part of our arms – over the main entrance and the Chapel, in the Old Dining Hall, on letterheads, Bursarial memorabilia, for sale and on the wrapped soap in your guest room.

These arms were the invention of Archbishop Parker in 1555, on the model of those at Abingdon where St Edmund was born, and described heraldically by the redoubtable Dr Alfred Brotherston Emden (the Abe) Principal 1929-51, as 'Or (on a field of gold) a cross patonce (splayed at the ends) cantoned by four Cornish choughs'.

The current Principal, Professor Michael Mingos FRS, introduced our two new stuffed real birds at a recent St Edmund's feast. They are really just crows, featured by Chaucer and Shakespeare after classification by Pliny the Elder and Linnaeus. There are two types, both with blue/black plumage and scimitar-like bills, but in the 'alpine' chough, flourishing in mountains all over the world, the bills and feet are yellow whereas in ours, the Cornish type, mainly found on the west coasts of Britain, both are red. They are particularly fond of cliff areobatics and – let's face it – thrive on dung insects; but regrettably, due to agricultural changes and bad weather, they died out in Cornwall in 1973.

But rescue is at hand. All the British chough people met recently in conference hitting the national press and there are two front-runners now active, although on different lines – the National Trust, who own 40% of the Cornish coastline, and the Rare and Endangered Bird Breeding Centre at Paradise Park, Hayle, with whom I got the College registered as 'Friend of the Chough' some eleven years ago now.

So may this volume of poems inspire them! Our first two identified Principals came from Cornwall – John and Robert Luc de Cornubia (1319-24) and the chough is surely part of our mystique. We must cherish it.

Arthur Farrand Radley
Hon Secretary Emeritus, St Edmund Hall Association

Fund-Raising Chough

To Cornish folks you were "The Market-Jew".
Of course. Yarmulka, hooded eyes below,
Black-jowled; perched on brushwood stool,
Crying your wares with raucous tone.

Some called you "Hermit Crow". Far-sighted.
Black habit, glinting under-hose,
Diet of worms your Lenten fare,
Aloof, recluse, dark misanthrope.

"One's unlucky – two's good luck,
Three for health and four for wealth"
The old rhyme runs. Maybe our crested patrons
Will lay for us a rich sustaining nest-egg...

Michael Cansdale
President of the S.E.H. Association

The old country names for the chough – "Hermit Crow" and in Cornwall "Market Jew Crow" – together with the old Essex rhyme, are given in C.E. Hare's *Bird Lore*.

xiv

Editorial Introduction

Although the Cornish chough is a familiar college emblem, few members of St Edmund Hall have ever seen a real one. So it was something of an event when the Principal displayed two of this species (stuffed and mounted in a glass-fronted box) at the Feast of St Edmund. I was not alone in being surprised by their appearance: they are very different from the stylised creatures who appear in our college coat of arms. Pitch-black, with red curved beaks and talons, they resemble birds of prey. The moment you see them, you imagine them in motion – scavenging for food on the cliff-side, or soaring free.

At our feast-night, the Principal gave an amusing account of the chough's 'acrobatic and over-friendly' antics. Drawing on the bird's heraldic significance for the Hall, he recited a poem by Dorothy Williams (included in Part Four of this volume) which pronounced the bird's name in various ways. ('Chuff' is of course the correct pronunciation.) After dinner, in the convivial atmosphere of the Senior Common Room, I suggested to Michael Cansdale that the Hall might produce a Christmas card commemorating the chough, with a picture and maybe one or two poems. Soon we found ourselves hatching a plot for a slim volume – to be timed for Christmas 2001, perhaps? – and in any event to be sponsored by the S.E.H. Association.

What started as a modest proposal grew more ambitious with time. I approached a number of published poets, to ask if they would make a contribution to our anthology as a way of supporting the Hall. To my delight, most of them turned out to have first hand knowledge of choughs, and were glad to contribute. The word soon spread; colleagues and friends joined in; and before long we had about a hundred original contributions. Some of the Fellows' poems were inspired by the Principal's speech on St Edmund night; others by the stuffed choughs themselves, which now nest in the Senior Common Room. Arthur Farrand Radley's article in last year's Magazine proved a valuable source of information; as did the website for 'pyrrhocorax pyrrhocorax' on the internet. Verse in every register, from the reverential to the flippant, poured in. Those who did not want to contribute poetry gave articles or short passages of prose. All sorts of illustration followed. In the end I had to be selective, or the book would have run to several volumes.

As it is, our anthology has six separate parts, each with its own introduction. In the first part (which includes Iain Bain's article on

Bewick's chough) are poems concerned with the bird's habitat and behaviour, as well as its status as an endangered species. The second, entitled 'Prophetic Birds', contains poems which play on the chough's literary and symbolic associations. The third part, with an introduction by Phil Cardinale, explores the chough's connections with Arthurian legend. The fourth part is a miscellany of poems, in a wide range of forms and registers. The fifth is devoted to the bird's significance for St Edmund Hall; and the sixth contains poems written collaboratively by some of the Hall's undergraduates. The illustrations for Parts One, Two and Three have been contributed by Lucy Wilkinson. Geoffrey Bourne-Taylor has illustrated Part Four; and Parts Five and Six contain illustrations by various hands.

Nearly all the contributors to this anthology are in some way connected with the Hall, either professionally or through ties of friendship. We are very grateful for the readiness with which these friends and colleagues have responded to the invitation to write for the Hall. It is a special privilege to include an article by Iain Bain (formerly Curator of the Tate); and a poem by Anne Ridler, who has long been associated with the senior common room through her husband Vivian. Sadly, she died just before the publication of this book.

Every constituency of the college is here represented, from the former Principal, current Principal, Fellows and old members, through to M.C.R. and J.C.R members, secretarial staff, and the Porter's Lodge. Our anthology bears testimony to the Hall's active commitment to poetry, and to the vibrant community of poets and poetry-enthusiasts who are teaching and studying in Oxford. The book appears at a moment in the Hall's history when we are looking to endow a second English Fellowship, so as to continue the Hall's longstanding tradition in this subject. If funds are successfully raised, the Fellowship will be named after Graham Midgley. But it is to the threesome of English dons, which also included Reggie Alton and Bruce Mitchell, that this volume is dedicated.

Lucy Newlyn
Fellow in English, St Edmund Hall

PART ONE
The Cornish Chough

Illustrations by Lucy Wilkinson

The Cornish Chough

Cornish choughs are larger than jackdaws and almost the size of crows. They fly along rocky coast-lines, foraging for insects, berries, dung-beetles, and grain. With their scarlet scimitar beaks and red claws, they are more striking than their alpine relatives. Yet it has been quite common for the name 'chough' to be used indiscriminately of birds in the corvine family. According to the Revd. C.A. Johns (FLS), a nineteenth century clergyman and ornithologist, 'the name Chough was probably in ancient times used as a common appellation of all members of the family Corvidae which have black plumage, this one being distinguished as the 'Cornish Chough' from the rocky district which it frequented.'

Known by their shrill cry ('kaa, kaa, kyaaa') and their sportive behaviour, choughs are gregarious creatures. Thomas Bewick in his *British Birds* even implied that they could be kept as pets. The chough, he said, 'is easily tamed, becomes extremely docile, and is very fond of being caressed, by those to whom it shows an attachment.' But 'its shrill notes and mischievous qualities render it a sometimes troublesome inmate. It also becomes bold and pugnacious, and resents an affront with violence and effect, by both bill and claws. It has a great aversion to strangers.'

In Bewick's time, choughs were still fairly common in the coastal regions of Britain. Gilbert White, in his *Natural History of Selborne*, reported on 8 October 1770 that 'the Cornish chough builds, I know, all along the chalky cliffs of the Sussex shore'. But a hundred years later, Kilvert made the following entry in his Diary for 22 July 1870:

> In one of the Serpentine shops of the Lizard there was a stuffed Cornish Chough. He is an elegantly shaped bird cleanly made with red or orange beaks and legs. He is very rarely found now even along the Cornish cliffs.

A lot happens to bird-life in a century. Choughs are now categorised among the rare and endangered species of the British Isles; and until last year it was believed that they had died out in Cornwall. None had been sighted there since 1973. A combination of agricultural changes and a succession of hard winters have made it difficult for them to find food; so they have been driven away to the wilder coastal regions of Ireland, Scotland and Wales. Sixty-five breeding pairs were recorded in Scotland in 2000, two thirds of them living on the Hebridean island of Islay. As Derwent May reported in *The Times* (26 February):

2

Apart from the geese, the most remarkable bird of Islay is the chough...I went off looking for them with the birdwatching owner of the Port Charlotte hotel. We went off on the sand-dunes on the western side of the island. Eventually we saw a large flock of rooks on a grassy hilltop just in from the sea, and among their calls we heard the shrill, gull-like cries of the choughs. Then we saw them, about 50, running in a separate flock beside the rooks, pecking with their curved bills, the biggest flock in Britain.

Because of the damage wreaked on their natural habitat (by pollution and the tourist industry), conditions in Cornwall are no longer propitious for the chough. But various practical measures are being taken to coax it to return home. This volume has emerged at an encouraging turning-point in the bird's history. On 21 May 2000, a headline appeared in *The Times*, announcing 'CORNISH CHOUGH RETURNS TO CLIFFS'. The Centre for breeding at Paradise Park has been training its captive birds in order to release them into the wild, where it is hoped they will flourish. This is one of a number of initiatives recently taken to ensure that choughs have a future in Cornwall. The National Trust aims to ban the use of pesticides and to improve the bird's chances of survival by increasing the amount of grazing land along the coastline. A local farmer, Francis Crocker, is re-creating the chough's favourite nesting-grounds on his land at Trevigue farm, Crackington Haven. Further afield, in Canterbury, there are plans to reintroduce the chough into the Kent countryside, where it was wiped out as early as the 17th century because an 'Acte for the Preservacioun of Grayne' decreed that 'every parish should provide nets for their destruction'. "Conservationists in the county have been working with their counterparts in Cornwall" reported David Sapsted in the *Daily Telegraph* (14 April 2001): "The first male chough has now arrived at the Wildwood animal sanctuary, just outside Canterbury, and David Gow, a conservationist heading the program, is looking for a female".

Recent set-backs (such as foot-and-mouth disease) have slowed down these attempts at progress. But we should not give up hope. One day this rare and beautiful bird may be as common as it was in Bewick's time.

L.N

Chough

Desolate that cry as though world were unworthy,
See now, rounding the headland, a forlorn hopeless bird,
trembling black wings fingering the blowy air,
dainty and ghostly, careless of the scattering salt.

This is the cave-dweller that flies like a butterfly,
buffeted by daws, almost extinct, who has chosen,
so gentle a bird, to live on furious coasts.

Here where sea whistles in funnels, and slaps the back
of burly granite slabs, and hisses over holes,
in bellowing hollows that shelter the female seal
the Cornish chough wavers over the waves.

By lion rocks, rocks like the heads of queens,
sailing with ragged plumes upturned, into the wind
goes delicate indifferent the doomed bird.

Rex Warner (1945)

Tar Chough

Marcus Woodd

Cornish Choughs (I)

The only pair I knew were a long way from home
In Gwynedd housing for a season
In a knacked bal[1] above a churchyard where
Among the locals following their trade
Dead of the dust were a few Tre, Pol and Pen.

David Constantine

1. A 'knacked bal' is an exhausted mine.

Choughs

I follow you downhill to edge
My feet taking as naturally as yours
To a sideways tread, finding footholds
Easily in the turf, accustomed
As we are to a sloping country.

The cliffs buttress the bay's curve to the north
And here drop sheer and sudden to the sea.
The choughs plummet from sight then ride
The updraught of the cliffs' mild yellow
Light, fold, fall with closed wings from the sky.

At the last moment as in unison they turn
A ripcord of the wind is pulled in time.
He gives her food and the saliva
Of his red mouth, draws her black feathers, sweet
As shining grass across his bill.

Rare birds that pair for life. There they go
Dive-bombing the marbled wave a yard
Above the spray. Wings flick open
A stoop away
From the drawn teeth of the sea.

Gillian Clarke (1997)

Birds of the Pie Kind

'The Cornish chough...frequents rocks, old castles, and churches by the sea-side, like the daw; and with the same noisy assiduity...These are birds very similar in their manners, feeding on grain and insects, living in society, and often suffering general castigation from the flock for the good of the community.' (Goldsmith, *Animated Nature*)

Nursed in a hair-nest,
inside a cradle of sticks,
inside a crevice
in a cave
sprayed salt stipple,
                    room enough
for five or six sickle beaks,
for a dozen or so blood-coloured shanks,
hair bones, skin breast sprouting quills.

Every day the sea swells nearer;
every hour another stay cracks. Red bills
snap at the envelope of light
scrabbling to break into the sun.

Only one will one day wonder
why it was so eager to be gone.

Fiona Stafford

Namanalagh

Somewhere in the pine trees beyond the lough
two stones are being knocked together
– once twice three times – though
I realize that this is not
in fact the case – it's a chough
I heard – it's clatt-
ery cry that's like the real hard stuff
poteen distilled on stony hills
where the black craychur
should be sounding its red beak
against the screes
not hiding out in the soft bog by the lough

Tom Paulin

23/11/00

Above: the first draft of Tom Paulin's poem 'Namanalagh'. Final version on page 9.

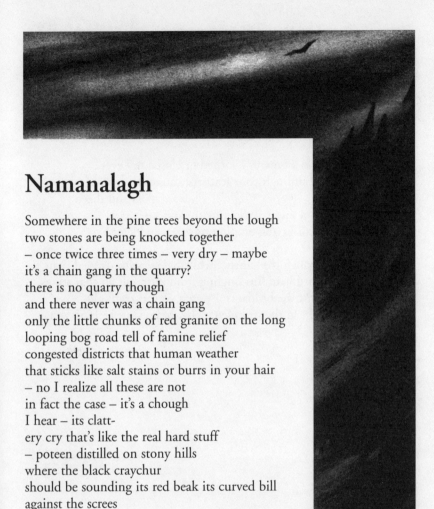

Namanalagh

Somewhere in the pine trees beyond the lough
two stones are being knocked together
– once twice three times – very dry – maybe
it's a chain gang in the quarry?
there is no quarry though
and there never was a chain gang
only the little chunks of red granite on the long
looping bog road tell of famine relief
congested districts that human weather
that sticks like salt stains or burrs in your hair
– no I realize all these are not
in fact the case – it's a chough
I hear – its clatt-
ery cry that's like the real hard stuff
– poteen distilled on stony hills
where the black craychur
should be sounding its red beak its curved bill
against the screes
not hiding out on the soft bog by the lough.

Tom Paulin

Metamorphosis (Chough in Flight)

Stilted in your decent black, slightly pompous daw,
proper as a dominie, with jerky clockwork walk,
maladroit and awkward, voice a dour laconic caw,
stiff on stems of sealing-wax, along the cliffs you stalk.

Careless for a moment, I turned or closed my eyes...
light rushed through your feathers, caught their mineral
                                      gloss and sheen
threaded on a thermal, floating up and up, to rise
tilting and curvetting on pinions sharp and keen,

shearing through the sunrise, while below, with dazzled sight,
wind-whipped hair, lips tingling from crisp salt air that stings,
braced against the brilliance I watch your dizzy flight,
breath caught in the turbulence that bears your arching wings.

Susan Reynolds

Bewick's Chough

The Chough
or red-legged crow
(*Corvus Graculus*, Linn. – *Le Coracias*, Buff.)

This bird is about the weight of the Jack-Daw, but of a taller and longer shape. The bill is long, curved, sharp at the tip, and of a bright red; the iris is composed of two circles, the outer red, the inner light blue; the eye lids are red; the plumage is altogether of a purplish violet black; legs red like the bill; claws large, hooked, and black. It builds on high cliffs, by the sea side, lays four or five eggs, spotted with yellow, and chiefly frequents the coasts of Devonshire, Cornwall, and likewise many parts of Wales: some are found on the cliffs of Dover,* and a few in Scotland. In a wild state it feeds chiefly on insects and berries. It is easily tamed, becomes extremely docile, and is very fond of being caressed, by those to whom it shows attachment, but its shrill notes and mischievous qualities render it sometimes a troublesome inmate. It also becomes bold and pugnacious, and resents an affront with violence and effect, by both bill and claws. It has a great aversion to strangers. Like the tame Jackdaw it is fond of glittering objects, and is equally mischievous, active, and restless. It examines everything, and is perpetually in search of insects. It soon learnes to eat raw or dressed meat, but will not eat common worms.

* ... "How fearful
And dizzy 'tis, to cast one's eyes so low!
The crows and choughs, that wing the midway air,
Show scarce to gross as beetles."

*   *   *

This engaging description of our emblematic Chough has been taken from the eighth edition of Thomas Bewick's much loved *History of British Birds*. First published in two volumes – the Land Birds in 1797 and the Water Birds in 1804 – it was to become the first truly popular English natural history. As children the Brontës pored over its pages and made copies of Bewick's remarkable engravings. In the opening of *Jane Eyre*, Charlotte Bronte describes her heroine sitting with the book on her knee, absorbed in its tail-piece vignettes – happy, fearing nothing but interruption. In later years Ruskin borrowed some of Bewick's drawings for his Oxford lectures in which he made great claims for him as a daughtsman; and Constable's biographer C.R. Leslie wrote of him in his *Hand-book for Young Painters* as being a truly original genius, 'who though not a painter, was an artist of the highest order in his way'.

A delightful example of the book's contemporary influence, apears in a letter Charles Kingsley wrote when cultivating an acquaintance with Bewick's daughters:

> When your father's book on birds ?rst came out , my father, then a young hunting squire in the New Forest, Hampshire, saw the book in London, and bought at once the beautiful old copy that was the textbook of my boyhood.. He, as sportsman and field naturalist, loved the book, and carried it up and down, in days when no scienti?c knowledge could be got – from 1805 to 1820; and when he was laughed at in the New Forest for having "bought book about dicky-birds" – till his fellow Squires, borrowing the book of him – agreed it was the most clever book they had ever seen, and a revelation to them – who had these phenomena under their eyes all their lives, and never noticed them.

In an extensive correspondence Bewick had many letters from amateurs of natural history – asking questions, sending specimens, pointing out errors. His energy was astonishing, for he was running a busy engraving business employing copperplate printers and three to five apprentices in his workshop. The preparation of his texts and the wood engravings for his books was the labour of evenings after the workshop closed, and letters from all over the country had to be answered at the same time – many were not 'post-paid', let alone welcome, and a week's worth of incoming post could cost a journeyman's wage Bewick wherever possible drew from a live subject. He kept a Siskin in a cage while he was making his preliminary drawing, and he had a Corncrake with an injured leg in a splint, running about his workshop ?oor and garden. The Chough, being an altogether rarer bird, he drew from a stuffed specimen in the collection of Marmaduke Tunstall of Wycliffe in North Yorkshire, where he stayed for a month in 1791. Perched on a ladder among the glass cases of this very early assembly of the taxidermist's art, he frequently had difficulty in getting a good view, and not always were the birds well set up. Often he put his subjects in appropriate and beautifully observed landscape backgrounds drawn with a painter's eye from a powerful memory. As legend had it that the soul of King Arthur took wing in the body of the Chough it would be pleasing to think that Tintagel could be seen in Bewick's clifftop castle, but his settings were seldom topographically precise.

After a preliminary pencil drawing, Bewick would sometimes make a finished watercolour as a guide to the tonal values to be translated into his monochrome engraving. The back of the drawing was leaded with a soft pencil and the outline of the figure was then transferred to the surface of a boxwood block by scribing with a fine hard point. The rest was freehand engraving with the tools of the metal engraver, working with a sureness of touch trained by more than twenty years of turning his

13

hand to every kind of image on copper, brass, silver and steel. The fine close-grained wood, worked on the end grain, was carefully prepared and cut to the height of type so that it could be put to press together with the text. To this was added the revolutionary technique of lowering specific areas of the block that were to carry those parts of the image, such as distant landsape and soft textures of feather, that by taking less pressure would thus appear grey. Well cared for, such blocks printed many thousands of impressions without wear, and the many that survive to this day, if dampened paper and the original press methods are used, print as well now as they did when first cut.

The descriptive texts in Bewick's *Birds* were a compilation drawn from earlier books such as those of Willughby and Ray, Pennant, and Albin, combined with personal observation of his own. As the various editions progressed changes were made. In the first edition, the translation of Buffon's *Natural History general & particular* was made use of in referring to the Chough's being 'attracted to glittering objects' and being 'known to pull from the fire lighted pieces of wood, to the no small danger of the house'.

By 1826, a friend and admirer, John F.M. Dovaston of Westfelton in Shropshire had begun to send Bewick copious notes towards the revision of the text, and it seems likely that his love of Shakespeare was responsible for the quote from *King Lear* which first appears in this last edition of Bewick's lifetime. Dovaston was an interesting figure, and Bewick's letters to him are among the most lively to have survived. As a serious amateur naturalist he set up elaborate feeding tables to assist his observations and he was the first to record the territorial habits of the Robin. When an undergraduate at Christ Church in 1801, he compiled a list of forty-two members of his notional 'Oxford Bird Club' and among the Crowes, Finches, Drakes, Nightingales and Sparrowes of New College, St John's, Christ Church, and Magdalene, were Cock and Swift of 'Edm[d] Hall' – but alas, no Chough. Dovaston himself was a 'Tolerated Member' along with others such as Larker and Ravenscroft.

For many, the supplementary tail-piece vignettes – used to fill the spaces at the ends of the descriptions – are a contant source of delight. In his intrduction to the 1826 edition of the *Birds*, Bewick wrote:

> When I first undertook my labours in Natural History, my strongest motive was to lead the minds of youth to the study of that delightful pursuit ... My writings were inteded chiefly for youth; and the more readily to allure their pliable, though discursive, attention to the Great Truths of Creation, I illustrated them by figures delineated

with all the fidelity and animation I was able to impart to mere woodcuts without colour; and as instruction is of little avail without constant cheerfulness and occasional amusement, I interspersed the more serious studies with Tale-pieces of gaiety and humour; yet even in these seldom without an endeavour to illustrate some truth, or point some moral ...

It was 'fidelity and animation' in the figures which placed Bewick's engravings head and shoulders above what had gone before, and it was partly the crudity of such works as Thomas Boreman's many times reprinted *History of Three Hundred Animals* that had been the early spur to his endeavours. The *tale*-pieces as he called them, often set in the Northumberland countryside and giving a vivid portrayal of the rural life of his time, were full of narrative content – a boy who can't read a sign leads a blind man into a river, while their dog takes the safe crossing; an ass rubs its backside on a tottering war memorial – of the crumbling inscription all that can be picked out are the words 'battle ... splendid victory ... immortal ...'. In the vignette of the small boys and their snowman, which accompanied the article on the Chough, there can be seen the words 'Esto perpetua' – a gentle warning to those who set store by false hopes.

Nothing has been said here of Bewick's childhood on the banks of the river Tyne where his father rented a small five-acre farm and a land-sale coliery and where his love of the natural world was firmly settled. Or of his apprentice years in the only metal engraving workshop in the city of Newcastle; or of his brief time in London as a wood-engraver, and his later twenty-year partnership with his former master, Ralph Beilby, with whom he produced a *General history of Quadrupeds* in 1790. But

Esto perpetua!

the memoir he wrote at the end of his life for his daughter Jane, and which tells of these things, has become a minor classic since its posthumous publication in 1862. Charles Kingsley in thanking his friend wrote:

> You and your friends in free kindness could not have devised a present more to my taste than Bewick's Autobiography. I have read it through, and am equally delighted and astonished at it. Brought up as I was on "Bewick's Birds" … I always held him to be a great genius in his own line, but I was not prepared to find him so remarkable a man in other respects – his temperance and thrift, his simple virtue, his sound and wide views on all matters political and social, astonish me as do the prophecies, if I can so call them, and none more than those on social and economic reform which has since been carried out…

The book went through four further editions before my own, published in the 'Oxford English Memoirs and Travels' series in 1975, which for the first time gave the full text of the surviving manuscript now in the British Library.

Iain Bain

Part Two
Prophetic Birds

Illustrated
by Lucy Wilkinson

Prophetic Birds

'Overhead go the choughs in black, cacophonous flocks –
Bits of burnt paper wheeling in a blown sky.
Theirs is the only voice, protesting, protesting.'
(Sylvia Plath, 'Blackberrying')

A number of the contributors to this volume are familar with choughs. Tom Paulin listens to their 'clattery cry' in Donegal; and according to Bernard O'Donoghue their 'cryking' can be heard off the beaten track 'on the southern sweep of the Great Blasket'. David Constantine remembers seeing three (in Gwynedd 'housing for a season'), and John Powell Ward clearly knows them of old: the bird-watcher in his poem notes with the accuracy of first-hand reportage that they 'enter their nests direct, like bullets./Then leave free-falling'.

However, bird-life invites speculation and myth-making, as well as careful observation. The belief that birds are closely associated with humans, and sometimes have human souls, has a very long ancestry – one in which the chough has its own distinctive place. According to Beryl Rowland, this was 'the bird which decked itself out in fine feathers but deceived no-one; and it was the tell-tale bird which informed the husband of his wife's infidelity.' For this reason, the chough has been associated with the detection of guilt. Chaucer's Wife of Bath alludes to this in passing, and so does Macbeth, on seeing the ghost of the murdered Banquo:

> It will have blood, they say; blood will have blood.
> Stones have been known to move and trees to speak;
> Augures and understood relations have
> By maggot-pies and choughs and rooks brought forth
> The secret'st man of blood.

Skilled in the art of uncovering guilt, the chough is a soothsayer, a tattler, a voice of conscience, and an eloquent barrister. Perhaps because it is so clever, this bird is not immune to suspicion. Various medieval writers have associated it with thievery (including Chaucer); and a number of other aspects have conspired to give it a bad name. Rowland's summary, in *Birds with Human Souls*, reads as follows:

> When tamed...the chough could be taught to speak, but
> its voice was never pleasing. Given wine to drink, the bird
> was 'lascivious above measure'. The chough's inadequacies

gave rise to special proverbs: gracculus inter musas (a chough among the muses) signified 'an unlearned man in the schooles'. Another proverb stating that choughs held their peace when the swans sang meant that 'when fooles are silent, then wise men may teach profitable things'. Their physical appearance... was often a bad portent, foretelling cold and rain or famine and sterility. Devils were known to have transformed themselves into choughs.

With its somewhat chequered past, the Cornish chough has proved a rich resource for poets through the ages. Our anthology taps into old traditions as well as contributing to new ones. This section begins by drawing on the chough's association with Celtic mythology and its rich Shakespearian resonances. Anne Ridler's haikus allude to the lines from *Macbeth* already mentioned, in which this bird is seen as prophetic. Reggie Alton has checked the number of times Shakespeare uses the word 'chough' and concludes that seven is 'a magic tally' for this vanishing species. His poem focuses on the famous scene (earlier invoked) in *King Lear* where Edgar leads his father, the blind Gloucester, to an imaginary cliff edge, and tempts him with the consoling possibility of suicide. The picture Shakespeare creates, through Edgar, is haunting for its visual accuracy, its fidelity to an observer's eye for detail. But all this is ironically undercut. What Edgar offers to the blind Gloucester is a fantasy, a poetic creation:

The crows and choughs that wing the midway air
Show scarce so gross as beetles. Half way down
Hangs one that gathers samphire, dreadful trade!

So vivid is Edgar's picture that the old man jumps (or rather falls), all of seven bathetic feet, and is saved by his experience from the ultimate sin of despair. This moving scene inspires a subtly allusive poem by a great Shakespearian. It also provides the opportunity for James Stafford, one of our youngest contributors, to experiment with re-writing the Bard. In his version of the scene, a chough appears in the middle of Edgar's speech, delivers some words of prophecy, then vanishes.

Choughs are Celtic birds, as is the mythology that has grown up around them. They are associated with King Arthur, whose soul is said to have migrated into one when he died. (See Phil Cardinale's essay, in Part Three). Some of this Arthurian mystique is present in Jem Poster's poem, which associates the chough with depopulated farmland in coastal Wales, and with the return of the dead:

> We stood
> in the fading light and listened to the breakers
> hammering the rocks below us; heard the ousted
> spirits sweeping back to claim their own.

Whether the choughs embody the spirits of the dead farmers, returning to re-possess their property, or a banished race, wreaking its revenge on humans, the sense of menace is palpable. It is an almost gothic poem, reminiscent of Hitchcock's 'The Birds'.

There can be little doubt that endangerment has added to the chough's mystique. W.B. Yeats once wrote:

> is there any comfort to be found?
> Man is in love and loves what vanishes,
> What more is there to say?
> ("Nineteen Hundred and Nineteen")

These lines express a poignancy that has resonated through twentieth century treatments of our threatened bird. Rex Warner, in 1937, described the chough as 'forlorn', 'hopeless', and 'doomed' – but also brave in its delicate indifference to destiny. John Powell Ward gives it a numinous aura, like the bird-watcher who observes that 'all best things are rare', and is himself a poet-priest with a heavenly destination. Nicolas Jacobs, who spends much of his time in Wales, confesses to never having seen a chough. In his poem, the bird is symbolic of rarity, even perhaps of impossible hope. He knows that to see it would be a spiritual epiphany. But it would also involve the recognition of something familiar:

still after long years unlightened, I fancy
I should know it well enough, as one might
love, or the sudden hope of making sense.

In Cornish, the chough is called 'An Balores', and has become a symbol
of Cornish cultural identity. The bird's threatened but defiant charisma
links it with the Cornish language, destined since the mid-eighteenth
century for extinction. David Constantine, in the second of his poems,
alludes through the chough to the decline of an entire culture:

Everything going, going, gone,
The tongue, the knowledge, the heraldic choughs,
The miner, the fisherman.

Attempts to revive Cornish peaked in the
mid-nineteenth century, but nowadays
knowledge of it survives only amongst a
very few Celtic specialists. For those who
reject the Queen's English, this erosion is
seen as symptomatic of a much larger
phenomenon. Tony Harrison, in his poem
'National Trust', speaks of the demise of Cornish
in strongly political terms. Alluding to the oppression of
tin-miners at Towanroath, he condemns 'those gentlemen who silenced
the men's oath/ And killed the language that they swore it in'. His poem
concludes with these angry lines, in which an authentic Cornish voice
speaks out, but needs translation into Harrison's own Yorkshire
vernacular for its full power to be heard:

The dumb go down in history and disappear
and not one gentleman's been brought to book:
Mes den hep tavas a-gollas y dyr
(Cornish) – 'the tongueless man gets his land took'.

Those Cornish words might well be a motto for the chough, whose
Celtic call is frequently used as a metaphor for the dissenting voice of
poetry. (See Sylvia Plath's lines, quoted as an epigraph to this
introduction). As we saw in Part One, Tom Paulin clearly identifies with
this 'black craychur', whose cry is 'like the real hard stuff – poteen
distilled on stony hills'. The bird's voice reminds him of the oppression
of Irish peasants, and of the 'long looping bog-road' which provided an
indigenous and poverty-stricken population with work and therefore
relief during potato-famine. In a sense this poem would fit as easily into
Part Two of our anthology as it does in Part One. Paulin's chough is
physically located, actually heard, and carefully observed. But it is also

21

symbolic: a bird of protest, deeply embedded in Irish history. Paulin even rebukes the creature for temporarily 'hiding out on the soft bog by the lough' instead of 'sounding its red beak its curved bill/against the screes'.

L.N.

Saint Edmund preaches outside All Saints in a rainstorm:

Two Haikus[1]

His cross a perch for
Those prophetic birds[2] with harsh
Voices and curved beaks,

Edmund's silver tongue
Moves heav'n to tears, while below
Spellbound, all stay dry.

Anne Ridler

1. Author's note: "Saints and their Symbols" informed me that St Edmund preached 'in the churchyard of All Halloes', and when it began to rain some of the listeners fled, and got wet, but those who stayed were dry. (Or *thought* they were?)

2. Alludes to *Macbeth* Act III, sc.V:
> Stones have been known to move and trees to speak;
> Augures and understood relations have
> By maggot-pies and choughs and rooks brought forth
> The secret'st man of blood.

Crows and Choughs

Come on, sir, here's the place; stand still. How fearful
And dizzy 'tis, to cast one's eyes so low!
The crows and choughs that wing the midway air
Show scarce so gross as beetles. Half way down
Hangs one that gathers samphire, dreadful trade!
Methinks he seems no bigger than his head.
The fishermen that walk upon the beach
Appear like mice; and yon tall anchoring bark,
Diminished to her cock; her cock, a buoy
Almost too small for sight. The murmering surge,
That on the unnumber'd idle pebbles chafes,
Cannot be heard so high. I'll look no more,
Lest my brain turn, and the deficient sight
Topple down headlong.

Shakespeare (*King Lear,* Act IV, sc.vi)

Census of the Russet-pates

William Shakespeare (as everyone knows)
would use a good name to death or to worse than
(knock twice and ask for Kate – pay Harry beforehand
 – or that macho Italian shrew keeper)
so there *you* are choughs. Seven times he names you
(not as often as sparrows or hawks,
but a magic tally for a vanishing bird)
and as you pass thieving, gabbling, chatting
from play to play I shall always remember you
silently winging the midway air,
downsized by perspective to beetles,
staffage in a virtual reality
raised by a virtuous son
to jump a credulous and fallen father
out of despair.

R.E. Alton

The Darkling Chough

EDGAR
Come on sir, here's the place. Stand still. How fearful
And dizzy 'tis to cast one's eyes so low!
The crows and choughs that wing the midway air
Show scarece so gross as beetles. Halfway down
Hangs one that gathers samphire, dreadful trade!

Enter Chough in flight

CHOUGH
Hark Gloucester, to the darkling chough.
Our chattering ranks
Feel your dread from the sockets of the rocks
Many miles from this place.
And had you eyes enough, or some fitful heavenly sense
To find our form at ten masts-a-length
You might see us then as ailing ink to vellum,
A dismembered coracle on a livid sea,
Instead of this wild sod which lines your tread.
Build all of your houses on this thing to pass
And you *shall* not drown under shock of grass.
By my russet pate and midnight pelt, beloved only of
The trapster and his luck whose impulse is born within –
Your servant shows you this false roof.
Your king shall come mottled in time enough
Away, alack! He hears not the chough.

Exit

James Stafford

Chough

When I saw you in Wales where I walked
with the dark haired boy whose love I craved
you tipped in the wind like a kite. Stalks
of dandelions twisted and craned
as we did, thrilled at the sight of your
rare black form as it questioned the sky,
the hills, the grass, asking why and what for.
You were the above and we below, our eyes,
wings, arms and lips, feathers, beaks, skin –
the sum of our parts on these hills, in this world –
your racing above to where might be heaven,
our feet on this earth, eyes looking at you,
naming you whole, making blackness be chough,
wanting to say it, as if plain words could be answers enough.

Victoria Field

Migrant

Chough: the red-legged crow, or any
bird of the genus Fregilus or Pyrrhocorax

Black-backed spirit carrier
glowing through letters like loops
of an element

No dictionary definition
can hold you:

cliff-top sentry, patroller
of coastlines, you watch
for danger, invasions, change

guard on the airwaves,
your accent, like scratches on stone,
dashed-off and eroded,

migrating from Viking
to Lundy, Fastnet and the Channel,

turns meaning as ploughs
turn earth

Ka, kaa, kyar

carrion feeder on beaches
searching our entrails
for birth: barrow-beguiled –

winging souls Westward
back to your wild.

Jenny Lewis

The Birdwatcher

A priest as well, and his hair blew about
Like a halo, his dog-collar a choke.
He preferred the moor for walks, but hedges,
Ditches, and the muddy ruts of a wet
Field in autumn could find him too,
On occasion. He liked that solitude.

Once, caught in a chance meeting,
I tried to impress. "Ponies on the bryn
Last week, an otter in the sea. And something
Odd on the cliff; a crow with red legs –
Was it? But the locals are bored
With all that now, they've gone so global."

No reaction; as if hearing wild hoof-beats.
"Sounds like a chough" he said, drily.
"They enter their nests direct, like bullets.
Then leave free-falling. Surprised you saw it.
I've seen some. But all best things are rare."
He walked away, still determined for sky.

John Powell Ward

30

And if, here

No, I never saw one, or should that be
have never seen one? True, before common time
and place left vision circumsised, I loved

their sometime haunts, the wind-shaven turf
sky-starred with squill at blackthorn time
a world above the unseen roil and thump

of the swell. But they must have been
all but gone before I came there, and if
by some grace they returned, would I be here

to see them? Yet perhaps, beyond constraint
of co-ordinates, beyond the vanishing
perspectives of wasted time, they are there

after all, where some ladder of light strikes
briefly through a slate cloud, scarcely on
this cliff, but catching perhaps the next,

or next but one. And if, here, for a moment,
a plumed sweep of jet, a dart of scarlet
bill, gave blunt observing keeness and fire,

still after long years unlightened, I fancy
I should know it well enough, as one might
love, or the sudden hope of making sense.

Nicolas Jacobs

The Cornish Coat of Arms

The arms of Cornwall county council depict fifteen gold balls set in a black shield. The shield is enclosed by alternating blue and white wavy stripes, which represent the sea surrounding Cornwall. To left and right of the shield are figures symbolising two important aspects of the county. A bearded fisherman represents its maritime connections, a tin-miner its mineral wealth and industrial heritage. Above the shield, the Cornish chough rests his red talons on a ducal coronet. The duchy of Cornwall has long been the inheritance of the Prince of Wales, as is the title Duke of Cornwall.

As emblems of Cornwall, these golden roundels originated in the arms of King John's son, Richard, Earl of Cornwall, and Count of Poictou. Explanations of their significance vary. According to one account they represent peas (poix) in punning allusion to Poictou. But legend also has it that they are bezants (current in Europe from the ninth century, and deriving their name from Byzantium) and that the sum of fifteen bezants was demanded by the Saracens for the return of an Earl of Cornwall captured during the crusades. The ransom money was raised by voluntary subscription throughout Cornwall. The motto 'One and All' which appears beneath the shield is thought to commemorate this joint effort. But it also tells of Cornwall's community spirit.

Information from C.. Wilfrid Scott-Giles, *Civic Heraldry of England and Wales*, (London: J.M.Dent, 1933).

Cornish Choughs (II)

Becoming heraldic is the kiss of death.
It means you were; and soon you never were;
You are fabulous. Not one girl nowadays
Can summon a unicorn he has gone so pale
And even the black and red bird, not a soul.

How quaint Map Terwun[1] looks in his Gorsedd robes
Grinning like a piskey. He had the knowledge
On the old tongue at his fingertips
Every inch from Land's end to the Tamar Bridge.
I've got his books in Oxford but it's not the same.

'One And All' was the motto and the fifteen bezants
Dwindling in the pattern five, four, three, two, one,
Everything going, going, gone,
The tongue, the knowledge, the heraldic choughs,
The miner, the fisherman.

David Constantine

1. Author's Note: Map Trewun 'Son of Trewun' is my father-in-law, who was a bard, and the poem largely derives from the coat of arms of Cornwall. (See facing page. L.N)

Back

We'd guessed already, of course – pressing between
the unruly hedgerows up lanes whose surface crumbled
beneath our boots; or stumbling
through bracken when the lanes gave out. And yes,
the signs were everywhere – the herds
of feral cattle on the hillsides, tractors
rusting in smothered gateways, the blank
stare of deserted farmsteads; but nothing
spooked us like the choughs, the dark hordes lifting
from the cliffs at our approach to wheel and cry
above our heads. We stood
in the fading light and listened to the breakers
hammering the rocks below us; heard the ousted
spirits sweeping back to claim their own.

Jem Poster

Chough Dunromin

Old redfoot-jackdaw, you know where
to pick your retirement home, drawn
by the artist's tax concessions
to the southern sweep of the Great Blasket
where Europe's tourists, safe in their fleeces
or Aran ganseys, cower against
the August squall. When the rain stops
they'll hear you, cryking behind them
somewhere off the moss-soft beaten track;
or, when the sun's come out again,
outside the clubhouse in Ballybunion
where you while away the summer afternoon
in the company of other shy exiles.
What taxman could make you out down there?

Bernard O'Donoghue

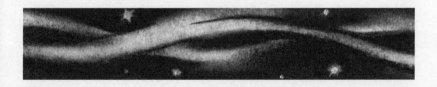

South African Sonnets

I

In the African bush – the light bright, air crackling,
Land red, umber, bleached, burnt-brown, still –
Our tracker, Joseph, points out Bataleur's eagle, sliding
Ominous in the updraft, above the plain, the lion kill.
'Black. Red legs. Red beak,' he announces – and I am back
At once on the Atlantic coast, waves combing, rough;
Grey, flat light, turf a block of emerald, rocks wet black.
A buffeting wind. Back with the tumbling, glossy chough.
Instead of the eagle's scream, seafarer, I hear the 'kee-ow'
Out of Arthurian mists of the slimline acrobat,
Clinging to the western margins, dream memory now.
Even Joseph, familiar with the unfamiliar, would blink at that,
And I could smile, magisterial, then kindly speak:
'Cornish chough, Joseph. Black. Red legs. Red beak.'

II

Robben Island, bleak, bland and flat, lies squat and bare
Like an English wartime aerodrome, except for the fiercer grey
Chill of its maximum security prison, a single storey,
Steel doors still clanging as pilgrim tourists shuffle by and stare.
On the shore, dabbing in the shallows, African oyster catchers, their
Straight, tube beaks and legs steeped in red enamel gloss.
Mandela will have seen these often on his way to mourn his loss
In the stark and blinding quarry's glare – too tired sometimes to care.
Arthur, after Camlann, they say, was changed into a chough
And the Welsh talk of him sleeping, ready, in a cave –
With Sobukwe, Sisulu, Mbeki perhaps, and others of the brave –
Labouring, dreaming, as the world grumbled gently, but not enough.
Sleeping saviours of the nation, birds, waiting not dead.
Chough. Oyster catcher. Rare. Black. Red.

John Trotman

The Orchard Underwater

Dragging for a place to catch the line,
I'm drawn back for a moment to the nearwater
by a clatter of choughs climbing off the headland
aiming somewhere for God.

                      This is no trick of aeronautics
but the genuine effect – God's Flyers, you called them,
            inking the air with trial after trial,
localised as downpour, a pencil of rain.

                             Yet,
what we remembered of these waters:
the cove in which the minke beached,
the pitchpoles of the bottle-nose,
one capsize, a storm or so; and
once, a raft of apples came
                bobbing round the bay –
we didn't know it then but they were
tipped into the sea by men
                  with memories of home,
a place that slipped away the year
            they dammed and sealed the valley floor,
an orchard sending up its fruit
                like life-floats or some SOS;
            – which might have been the last of it,
but some time on, in bony drought,
                  the lane rose from the lake,
and folk came from their homes again
                to walk among themselves;
past cattle pens, apple pots, the schoolroom
    trapped with fish;
        like time given back, offered over again;

as if all the words they failed to say
were spilled out on the quay and claimed
like undelivered letters finding home;
                              as if
we'd tapped our own lost tongue,
and stirred it into flight;
                        as if the sea
was rolled-up like a carpet on the hillside,
and the sun had scissored out the sky
                              and left it to one side,
and we had all the world to patch together
                                    in whatever order,
some fuzzy-felt, or stickle-brick
                        to set out as we'd choose it;
as if my steps could be with yours, as if we could
forgive ourselves, and take some second chance
before the rains
                    re-close on the chapel yard
and all I can taste is a crab hand of apples;
all that I see, that unkind flight to God;
all that I hear, the eerie tide
        of a church bell moving in the swell,
                    calling the waters to prayer.

                                        Matthew Hollis

This Place Perched

She nests in deep fissures, in caves
And performs easily acrobatics on the wing
So an inward looking to a graveyard terrain was not
The view she had in mind when she came to this valley
It was to have been temporary anyway
And she had committed herself to be an elegant stand-in
For a more colourful variety
Of a more predatory Oxford bird

There have been times she has been glad of the post
Even though a symbol and stationary
She watches carefully
The passing of a history
A slow maturing
Under archways
Counts the youth of many
And preens at their successes

However gleeful
The portentous moment proudly worn
However serious
Her assumption of the charge
Of looking over lives
Learned and intense
Even these best cultivated flowers
In their English glory
Cannot prevent

Soft dreams of flying
Over molten, heavy seas
Soaring with a vivaciousness
Only made possible
By the largest horizon
The biggest sky
The scent of salt

Sylvia Vance

Bird Witan

On this bleak edge
We're gathered now.
Cold starlight
Casts on glint of eye,
On curve of beak.

The question comes. "How long?"

"Ten years or so. Not more."

Dry rasp of feathers as I speak.

"Corncrake went last year.
Bunting too, but not without a fight.
Skylark, swift, in danger.
Even sparrow under siege."

A sigh. "None safe, I fear."

The mood moves with the speaking-stick.
The voice is deeper now:
The chough will speak.
Penumbra turns his red legs grey,
Each bird reduced to shadow-black,
All colour drained from land and sky.

The night reduces all to form against the void.

He speaks alone, with sombre lilt:

"Our rough hills and cliffs will still remain.
We shall continue till the sun burns cold
And earth to desert then returns.
We are the brothers of great Wodin's bird."

Hilly Cansdale

Chough Strays South

Damask's hiss. The clinking of little
glasses no taller than my beak;

tawny-eyed kittens in baked courtyards,
burrowing and sucking, and young girls

larking down marbled passages,
skipping morning school; dance-lines

of palm-trees practising curtsies,
the sips and kisses of dazed water.

All this and the sounds lamb-clouds
do not make. A buttercup moon.

Even the gulls sweet-talking, untuned
to my indigo, angry-mouthed sea.

What would I not do...I'd loop the loop
for one chill updraught, a single yelp.

Kevin Crossley-Holland

PART THREE Arthurian Choughs

Introduction
Phil Cardinale

Illustrations
by Lucy
Wilkinson

The Cornish Chough in Arthurian Legend

"YET some men say in many parts of England that King
Arthur is not dead, but had by the will of our Lord Jesu
into another place; and men say that he shall come
again..."   – *Sir Thomas Malory*, c. 1470

An old legend of Cornwall holds that, prior to his coming again, King
Arthur exists in the form of a chough. In his final battle Arthur killed his
illegitimate son Mordred with a spear and received a mortal wound in
return. Yet the King did not die, nor did he quite live, borne away on a
barge to the isle of Avalon by Morgan Le Fay, but rather by some magical
art his soul migrated into a new body of glossy black plumage, blood-red
talons, and a curved beak. Here he remains in some senses both alive and
dead, and will return in England's hour of greatest need.

This story in its earliest form is told by the errant knight Don Quixote
in Cervantes's tale, where it explains why Englishmen never harm this
bird. In this and many versions, Arthur's chough – technically a crow – is
called a raven. The terms appear to have been largely interchangeable well
into the eighteenth century, when the great naturalist Linnaeus referred to
Cornish choughs as "Hoopoe fire ravens." The legend of Arthur's
transfiguration is likely associated with the Celtic war goddess Morrigan,
from whom Morgan Le Fay is thought to derive. Morrigan could
transform herself into a raven or crow and in that guise watched battles
and sometimes influenced their outcomes by whipping warriors into
frenzies, and afterwards in avian form she pecked clean the dead to prepare
their souls for rebirth. One can imagine Celtic warriors in Arthurian times
checking the tide of battle by watching where these birds flew on the field.
Another influence upon this legend could be the cult of Mithras, wherein
the raven was the lowest of seven ranks through which a worshipper could
ascend. Perhaps most fundamental, however, is the special niche that the
chough's class of birds occupies in mythology world-wide.

Corvids, birds of the family of ravens and crows, were perceived in
almost all ancient cultures as originally white creatures who experienced
a fall. Jewish legend relates that Noah released a white raven from the ark
(before the dove) to test the waters, and God blackened it and
condemned it to eat carrion because it failed to return. The Greek Apollo,
wrestling the Python of Delphi, was told of a lover's infidelity by a crow
and blackened it in anger. Apollo then killed the woman, Coronis, and

out of his repentance came the birth of Asclepius, god of medicine. From the banana groves of Kilimanjaro, where sacrificial meats rolled downhill by dwarves are said to transform into ravens, to the Japanese isles, where crow-like beings known as *Karasu tengu* assist tornado makers, corvids paradoxically appear as both demiurges and destroyers. In European myth they are most often helpers and incarnations of deities, such as the ravens kept by the Norse god Odin (which Odin could shapeshift into), while amongst North American Indians 'Raven' is the great creator of the world and also its great trickster. At the most basic symbolic level, Raven represents appetite (hence the term 'ravenous'), a force which tends toward destructive excess yet nevertheless, and sometimes even despite itself, shows humans the way toward a good life.

The corvid's mystique still persists strongly, as evidenced by Edgar Allen Poe's "Raven" (after which an American professional football team has been named) and 1990s Hollywood films about the comic superhero "The Crow," an undead musician who becomes an avenging angel after he and his lover are murdered. These films follow a common pattern in which out of the corvid's fall, like that of the phoenix, there arises a potentially healing force. In augury, this bird's contrary meanings as a portent of either doom or divine providence figure prominently in British folklore. Most recognise the corvid as the bleak scavenger against whom farmers erect scarecrows, but behind this is a lesser-known protective kinship. A single black bird is a bad omen, superstition says, but two signify peace and plenty. (Famously, pairs are often monogamous throughout life.) Ravens with clipped wings kept at the Tower of London are in some sense guardians of the realm; when they depart, legend says, the monarchy will fall. While Shakespeare's chough is a troublesome tattler, on Medieval armour this bird signified "watchful activity of friends" and "stratagems in battle." Contemporaneous with its connection to Arthurian lore, the Cornish chough developed strong links with Canterbury's archbishops, particularly Thomas a Becket and his near successor, St. Edmund of Abingdon.

Anyone who sees a wild chough today cannot doubt why the old Cornish dubbed this extremely sociable and acrobatic bird the "King of Crows." As Rex Warner put it in *Poems and Contradictions* (1945):

This is the cave-dweller that flies like a butterfly,
buffeted by daws, almost extinct, who has chosen,
so gentle a bird, to live on furious coasts.

In Warner's poem the Cornish chough's rarity in modern times makes it into a flying contradiction – delicate yet fierce, ghostly yet vital. Yet the bird's near demise in Britain, and its celebrated 'coming again' recently to Cornwall's seaside cliffs, merely accentuate the image it has forever held. A fallen mediator between the living and dead, it is the prophetic creature that historical Knights of the Round Table would have seen overhead during battles, and whom they trusted would either inspire them to victory or else protectively devour their remains. This type of bird was in primeval man's first thoughts about the origins of the world, with its beak and talons poking into both regeneration and apocalypse. Today more than ever the Cornish chough seems a fitting vessel for the watchful spirit of Britain's once and future king.

Phil Cardinale

A Legend of King Arthur (at Sennen)

Headland of battle, long as choughs can fly –
The birds with beak and talon wet with blood,
As long as Genvor rears her raven brood
To croak against the Dane, the victory
Of those nine Cornish kings can never die;
No mill-wheel turns to-day with crimson flood
But all who round the Table-man take food
Must pray that Arthur's time again were by.
For once Excalibur with gleaming brand
Flashed hope to friend, confusion to the foe,
But Athelstane on Bollait's fateful field
Stamped British hearts to dust that could not yield,
And Arthur now on wings of night must go,
A deathless chough about a conquered land.

H.D. Rawnsley (1887)

Hidden

I have questioned people in every part of Cornwall in which king Arthur has been reported to have dwelt or fought...I have been told that bad luck would follow the man who killed a Chough, for Arthur was transformed into one of these birds.

Robert Hunt, FRS, Popular Romances of the West of England (1865)

Not that you'll see one now, but DO NOT SHOOT IT.
That bird might be just father of his nation:
One chough turns over plans for Restoration,
Biding his time, wheeling a sparse Atlantic.

Sometimes, monarchs do this: their loves profess
But kindly leave the stage.[1] And thus obscured,
The black heart of our once and future bird
Beats absolute in the charm of being powerless.

Still, attendant, we make correct obeisance
Before our hidden kings. Oh, we're good to them:
This waiting's just a trick to pull off absence.

Christ, barely risen, stiff still from the tomb,
Trudged off to Emmaus with shaken men
Who couldn't find the words, while he kept mum.

Seamus Perry

1. Though obscurity's the plan, a king's a king:
   So mufti then; but keep the scarlet stocking.

Metempsychosis[1]

Lost heralds, outriders of a vanished
race. Beaky, black-coated, melancholy;
eyes like hard drills that could bore
a hole from here to Land's End,
keen and cruel with intent.

Kyaa kyaa kyaa: a Celtic cry.
At night their trapped souls travel west, flap free
on the Cornish coastline, ride the rough wind sea-
ward, turn with the tide's turning, fly inland.

'What saw you there?' said the king.
'Sir', he said, 'I saw nothing
but the waters wap and waves wan.'[2]
Over Camelot the spirit soars
and slackens, spent.

Lucy Newlyn

1. Metempsychosis: a Greek word, meaning the transmigration of souls.
2. These lines are a direct quotation from Malory's *Morte D'Arthur*. They record the
dying king's last conversation with Sir Bedivere.

Chough (Coracia pyrrhocorax)

Considering their distribution in old haunts
Of armadas where even the people
Can bear an Iberian look, I'd like to believe
These crazy *kiaow-k'chuf* kazooers embody souls
Of red-lipped girls descended from flamenco dancers,
Or Catalonian cross-dressers in black skirts and
Red stockings, fled from the Inquisition,
Castanets clacking, castaway to flirt on cliffs
And strut their stuff above the wrecked Atlantic.

Though the authorities say the truth is other and
A while after all roads led to Caesar's Rome,
Or Ovid's exile, the soul of King Arthur
Migrated into one, which would as well explain
Why choughs are so fay and flighty, being
Deranged and déraciné just like me, with
My binocular visions, captive to a dream
I have lost and gained in being here before them
This day beside myself with pleasure?

Andrew McNeillie (2000)

The Graduate

Another walks past, stares like I'm that time of year
When I'm dying or dead
Says something to the other I can't hear.
Thorough plegm, thorough gin, still in my head
There is your song though. Bare ruined choirs where
Late the sweet birds sang. Bet they don't know I
Know that – or where it's from. Sod them, don't care.
Another talks past, just like you as you fly,
Arthur. Bet you didn't know I knew that,
With my alf a bottle and matches, king-size.
No fags though, ask, what are they laughing at?
Try to retort, another gawks past: wide eyes.

This I perceive, which makes your voice more strong,
Another walks past, and more shall ere long.

Ben Burton

Morte Arthur

'Corpus domini nostri
sanguine domini nostri
in vitam eternam. amen '

So sit down by steel graves
Rent greaves at bent plate
Humbled by fate.
At your back the shadow fails
                    falls
Then drags on the plain.
The sun splits red and bleeds to fade,
With red beak the black bird calls
For your name.

And for what now is that cup
Rim filling crimson
Clutching, spilling; drink deep
Swallow O swallow then sleep
Teeth stained red and feet.
you will come again.

But not in the woodsong fog
And the woodthrush call
By still waters of the winedark lake
Lapping the white-clear arm
Ice-carved, ash-tall
which you have not. Take
to the frayed night
And make for the tatters
Of what you have left
And wait.

For on the crimson mound forever
Will sway three aspens dear
And in their gold cages harmony hear
The woodthrush song and
The swallow call and
The dirge of the chough

And you need no fear (but love)
Through the grace of the dove
Your own dirge i hear;
Vouchsafed for thee.
All but (my God!).

You betrayed me.

David Milsom

Author's Notes

Title and Epigraph:
The possessive is removed from Malory's 'Morte d'Arthur' as this would have been too restrictive a title. The epigraph refers to the Eucharist, identifying the speaker as Christ, and predicting sacrifice and resurrection.

The First Stanza
The scene in Malory describing the Doomsday plain where Mordred had been defeated, at the point where the raven army of Yvain arrives. Dying, Arthur metempsychoses into the chough.

The Second Stanza
The chalice appears as part of the Grail legend, the indirect cause of Doomsday and the Eucharist. Christ asks Arthur within the chough to drink and complete the act of transubstantiation. This fuses with clasical mythology through reference to *The Wasteland* (Eliot in his atheist phase) and the re-birth of Procne and Philomela. The speaker concludes the stanza with a divine absolute certainty.

The Third stanza
Alludes to the Eliot's poem 'Marina' (which post-dates his conversion to Christianity) and the stichomythia of Shakespeare's 'Pericles' and Seneca's 'Hercules'. The 'winedark lake' involves the charged instant where one-armed sir Bedivere casts Arthur's sword Excalibur into the lake, where it is caught by the lone rising arm of the lady. It is only on the third attempt that Bedivere can commit to relinquishing the blade, betraying Arthur twice before he does so.

The final stanza
Evokes Hopkins's 'Binsey Poplars'. And 'Carrion Comfort' as well as 'The Wasteland'. The aspens imitate the three crosses on Golgotha. The 'gold cages' are at once sybilline and a natural phenomenon. The three birds who are all symbols of re-birth are encapsulated in the grace of the dove. The dirge is the Lord's prayer. In the last lines Arthur usurps Christ as speaker, but shows the suffering of Christ in him, as his plaint echoes the scene in Gethsemane. Thus the last lines betray the Christian reader who should hold faith and accept the truth, not be led astray by the voice of the neurotic priest; for the parentheses return to their earlier counterparts, stressing the casting aside of fear and doubt and the embracing of love.

PART FOUR
Chuffed

Illustrations by
Geoffrey Bourne-Taylor
and others

Chuffed

'Chough' is a comically undignified name, inviting the pun 'chuffed' and its twin, 'stuffed', as well as some more or less predictable rhymes – enough, tough, duff, buff – all of which make their appearance in this part of our collection. Several of the contributors have found surprising visual rhymes: lough, plough, cough, bough, dough. But this bird is not just a source of ingenious word-play. It has inspired a wide spectrum of themes and registers, in forms as various as lyric, dramatic monologue, free verse, rhyming couplet, verse dialogue, doggerel, clerihew, riddle, haiku, and limerick. English is not the only language represented in this and the next section of our anthology. We have a poem in modern Greek, one in French, one in Latin, and one in Japanese. Bruce Mitchell has contributed his first Anglo-Saxon riddle, together with a translation.

L.N.

Untitled

When I see a one-eyed chough
I pity birds whose life is tough.

When I see a two-eyed chough
I reckon God has done his stuff.

When I see a three-eyed chough
I start to think my eye-sight's duff.

When I see a four-eyed chough
I know that I have had enough.

Terry Jones

MICELES FORME RÆDELLE

```
Mid Creacum findest þu    min cnosl geolufete,
in heam Alpum   ond in Himalayum
na sunsciene swa ic    salwigfeþera
mid readum scancum    ond readum nebbe
ond mid ieþrum sange.    Þa Ælfred cyning weold
wlance Westwealas    witon me ær ic ferde
to windigum sænæssum    sæliges Yrlandes.
Ac cierre ic nu.   Chaucer ond Shakespeare
ymb me in leoþum sungon.   Leof eom ic in Cente
cradole in Englalonde   Cristendomes and in Healle
Halges Eadmundes.   Heard sceolde rædelle
ac samwis eaþe mæg    secgan hwæt ic hatte.
```

Mitchell's first riddle

You will find my yellow-footed relatives among the Greeks, in the high Alps and in the Himalayas. They are not handsome like me, with my dark plumage, red legs and red beak, and more pleasant song. In the reign of King Alfred, the proud people of Cornwall knew me before I went off to the windy seacliffs of blessed Ireland. But I am coming back now. Chaucer and Shakespeare sang of me in verse. I am loved in Kent, cradle of Christianity in England, and in St Edmund Hall. A riddle should be hard to solve but you don't have to be very bright to guess what I am called.

Bruce Mitchell

Chough and the Gossip-Mongers

We abhor this spin. All this word-puff.
Our lives were clean and picked, rough-
housing it here on this glistening bluff.

First some doctor hinted, 'just off the cuff',
that the Bear-King never snuff-
ed it and flies high with us. Guff!

As if that weren't enough,
academics and poets soon began to truff-
le for little bits of fluff.

No peace after that. Old Malory the Gruff
was right: nasty gossip-mongers, luff-
ing up and half-drowning in air, cuff

us with their quackery and, worse, cause suff-
ering. Tough them out! K'chuf!

Kevin Crossley-Holland

Haiku

A chough clears its throat –
splays the nib of his bill, makes
a mess of the sky

Antony Dunn

Chuff Chuff. Chuffing. Chuffed. Chough

Chuff chuff is the Choo-choo
theThomastheHenrytheEdward, theThomastheHenrytheEdward,
Chugging in the child's mind
And silent steamless sidings.

Condemned by the dictionary
To near obsolescence,
The plain talking Northener
*****ing well hopes not.

Chuffed is the housewife
Who notes, when it matters,
That her emmental souffle
Has risen rather nicely.

The chough is the black,
The red-stepping, cruel-pecking, cliff-dwelling bird.
No crow. No raven. And no bloody jackdaw.
Often forgotten, but here not ignored.

But if the 'chough' is the 'chow'?
Enough, for now.

Natalie Parker

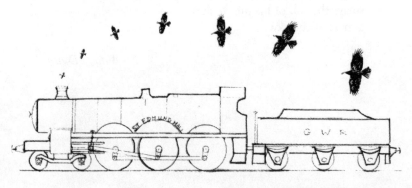

Illustration by Bill Williams

Tough Chough

chough	proud
	too loud
chough	puffed
	too chuffed
chough	gruff
	too rough
gun	aimed
	chough maimed
	red legged it
tough	pegged it
chough	dead
nuff	said

anon

Tick Tock
Squawk

I'll make this poem succinct,
for the chough is nearly
extinct.
If you eat one for your dinner,
why then you're an evil sinner.
Black defier of laws
geometric:
don't hurt it with your
electric
pylons.
Dry ones, in a jar,
will never fly as far
as moist fresh alive ones.

Mike Tweddle

Icarus dicare chough

To write a poem about a chough

(with apologies to Jacques Prévert and William Carlos Williams)

To write a poem about a chough, first design a cover for
The British Book of Choughs, then put it on the shelf beside
The Big World Book of Hens. Now introduce the two.
Place some worms by them and wait. If you are lucky,
one or other of these books will boldly or will gingerly
creak open to release a claw, leg, thigh, wing, breast, neck,
and lastly eye and beak. or possibly vice versa.
If after several days no bird has yet appeared,
take both books, gently, put them, with fresh worms, and corn,
inside a red wheelbarrow. Wait until the rain has stopped.
surely, now, white chickens, and a large black chough or two,
will flutter to the ground. And there will be a poem.

Judy Tweddle

Thomas Chatterton to Thomas Rowley, 24 August 1770, Redcliffe, Bristol: A Verse Epistle

Magpies steal. This was not stealing. My self
From myself estranged, I borrowed you.
I wore your monkish cowl as my disguise.
Your parchment, quill, you lent me willingly.
Willingly you lent me language too.
A novice still, I trained myself to speak
In a strange tongue. Across the years, the centuries,
Lost words and vanished sounds revived in me.
In me came alive an antique world no-one
Had ever known. Your habit fitted me.
Your speech I made my own.

I am before, I am after, I am behind my time.
Until my hour comes round, all time disowns me.
By neglect, by poverty, I am undone.
My place, my name, forsake me.
But this I know, this I foresee:
That, like our noble king,
Bird-shaped and black-hooded, fiery-beaked,
I will haunt this land, unrecognised
Save only by the trusted few.

Here in my garret, once your cell, you
To your self I willingly resign. Your signature,
Your quill, your parchment, I forego.
Here begins my glory, my posterity.
I drink deep from this chalice. I compose
my fame. I fling my arm down, so.

Editor's Note:
Thomas Rowley was the fictional fifteenth century poet and monk whose poetry Thomas Chatterton forged. On 24 August 1770, Chatterton allegedly committed suicide by taking arsenic. Recent scholarship has questioned the traditional account of his death. But this, his final poem, suggests that a deep melancholy led to his taking his own life. The address from which the poem was written is both biographically and symbolically significant. St Mary Redcliffe was the church in which Chatterton claimed

to have discovered a chest containing the original manuscript of *Felix Farley's Journal*, a passage of pseudo-archaic prose. There is also a clear metaphorical linkage between the 'red cliffe' of the church and the chough's habitat and colouring. Chatterton's tragic and heroic identification with our Arthurian bird is spelt out in lines 17–20. The poet alludes to his garret as a cell (line 21) because he has confused his own identity with that of the monk Rowley. It is possible that Chatterton also associated himself, via the persona of Rowley, with a third Thomas: St Thomas Becket, who died a martyr and whose arms bore a trio of choughs. (The stance of martyrdom was a well-established trope during the eighteenth century for the neglected poet;, especially amongst minor writers.) Ironically, of the three figures linked associatively through their Christian name in this verse epistle – Rowley, Becket, and Chatterton – only the fictional Rowley achieved immediate recognition. Just as Becket's arms were awarded posthumously (after his assassination at Canterbury Cathedral), so Chatterton only became famous after his sensational death.

This poem is as remarkable for its prescience as for the intensity of its self-pity. In it, Chatterton correctly prophesies that he will achieve an afterlife. He also predicts that what will most impress future readers is not his poetry (which is rarely read) but the manner of his dying. In his final triumphant line the poet prepares the way for his reception at the hands of readers and illustrators for centuries to come. See for instance James Wallis's famous oil-painting (1856) which is housed in the Tate. Geoffrey Bourne-Taylor has caught the same moment of death with his Gothic rendering of Chatterton's metamorphosis from man to chough.

Ork?

It's a rare old bird
and no-one's ever seen it
(excepting yourself)
– not for centuries at least
and you come along and say
you "spotted it in a tree"
– nice touch that *spotted* –
roosting, no less, on an egg
so big it made the branches creak,
an egg as big as a ton of marble
and as smooth. The tree
was perfumed and waxy-leaved
and like the bird and its egg,
you say, one of a kind.
Just taking a stroll
were you, and there it was?
Well, the description fits
but you could've dug that out
of some medieval bestiary
It's name, too, escapes you.
Ork you tried and said it wasn't.
Not crow. Not roc. Not rook. Not awk.
You'd better find that bird again
and this time a roll of film
and, yes, some map-coordinates
wouldn't go amiss
because "a bower in Araby"
– or was it Aramaspia? –
is not so much a signpost
as a wild goose chase.

Jamie McKendrick

Song

A bird dressed proud in red and black
Upon my window sill
Did stand and sing to me one day
In beautiful rhyme, until
The bell within the tower tolled,
Time shook his melody,
The bird took flight to land untold,
Left nought but misery.

Ben Burton

A Mid-Term Clerihew

Arthur Hugh Clough's
Poem about choughs
Proved far better than mine
Especially in the concluding line.

Fiona Stafford

The Last Chough in Cornwall

Scene: St Ives Police Station

" Good morning, Constable,
I've brought this in."

" What is it –
A Blackbird? "

" It's the last Chough
to be found in Cornwall –
all black with red beak and legs
– I'm handing it in for
Safe Custody
(so that it doesn't escape)."

" Right, Sir,
I'll just pop it under
this
Police Helmet,
(so that it cannot escape)."

" Thank you; good day."

" Sarge,
There's a helmet on the counter
underneath which
I have placed
The-Last-Chough-in-Cornwall
– all black with red beak and legs
(so that it will not escape);
What should I do now? "

" You, a Graduate Entrant?

Why, the next thing is to tie a
Property Label
to one of its
Little Red Legs!
(but don't let the blighter escape)."

" 'ave you done that,
Constable Trelawny
(or have you let it escape)? "

"Yes and No, Sarge,
but I've crushed every bone in its body. "

Geoffrey Bourne-Taylor
(Ex PC 134N)

Acrobatlike Batlike

Patrick Williams

Chattering

aerobatic black shadow hordes
swoop from low bough
swing in flight high
loop in sky light
through
air.
air
blue
veer in sky sheer
sweep to granite height
show in air light acrobatlike batlike
blood beaked
petrol jet plumed
chough

Elizabeth Scott-Baumann

Six and a half ways of listening to a chough[1]

The chough sits motionless
Black is the silent colour

The chough flew over the Oxford train
Chuff

Gowned dons in the quad
A cabal of choughs

'The thef, the chough', says Chaucer
He could talk

Odes are for sweet birds
Skylarks and nightingales
The creaking chough
Sings unsung

Sonnets are for lovebirds
Clinch in a couplet
Free and numberless the chough

What is the sound of one wing flapping?

Priscilla Martin

1. Alludes to Wallace Stevens's poem, 'Thirteen Ways of Looking at a Blackbird'.

赤い靴　熊に残して冬の空

AKAIKUTSU KUMANI NOKASHITE HUYUNOSORA

AKAIKUTSU	:	Red shoes
KUMANI	:	With the bear
NOKOSHITE	:	Leaving behind
HUYUNOSORA	:	The winter sky

(Japanese haiku by Arihiro Fukuda)

"Having left behind their red shoes with the bear, [they must/might have flown into] the winter sky [and disappeared]."

Winter Sky

Gone. Vanished into thin air.
Their red shoes are where?
Left behind with the bear.

(English version by Lucy Newlyn)

The White-Winged Chough

I got the bird-book, looked right through,
And found it. It's a White-winged Chough.

I saw it sitting on the plough –
I think it was a White-winged Chough.

I'm not quite certain, though,
It might have been a White-winged Chough.

And yet I'm not quite sure enough,
To label it a White-winged Chough.

I tried to name it, got a cough,
And out it came as white-winged Chough.

But is my reading really thorough?
Could it just be a White-winged Chorough?

No, no! I gave it careful thought.
Of course it's not a White-winged Chought!

A Choo, A Choe, a Chow, a Chuff –
Or even Choff – I've had enuff!

I'm in a Slough of Despond now –
What's that again? Yes, I said slowgh!

Or is it Sloo, Sloff, Sluff, or Sloe?
PASS me the dictionary – DON'T THROWGH!

Dorothy Williams

Stuffed Chough

There's something awkward and askew
About this sleek black chough
Red beaked and glass-eyed in the case
But still a bit of rough

Although I've never seen one fly
Suppose that like a crow
You'd flop against a clear blue sky
And struttle in the snow.

Mina Gorji

the anglo-saxon

blackbird spiralled,   spoke with beak
head held high,   honouring home,
lord's life-house,   light of love,
song of soul,   soared in sky.

Ben Burton

Vers Libres on stuffed choughs

A brace of chough in a battered box.
Just a hint of habitat:
sparse grasses, and a bit of grit.

Rakish beaks gore-burnished brown,
bloody legs beneath their gown,
they hunt soft targets in their turbid loughs
or with their pointed pinions' sable sleeves
slash indecipherable zig-zags through a painted sky.

Softly, but perceptibly, they croak,
counter-passant in their case,
of other colleagues getting stuffed.

Christopher J. Wells

Two Choughs in a Black Hole

Bill Williams

Ough

Once I saw a little	chOUGH
Sitting on a woodland	bOUGH
It pecked upon a bit of	dOUGH
Which gave it quite a nasty	cOUGH

Carol McClure

A Neoclassical Curse

(Nearly) every schoolboy knows
that *Go to Hell* in ancient Greek
is *why not hie thee to the crows?*

But possibly he does not know
that *chough* in Greek is *fiery crow.*
And so,

if *Go to Hell*'s not strong enough
recall the flaming feet and beak
and mutter *Hie thee to the chough.*

Hazel Rossotti

PART FIVE
Teddy Hall Choughs

Illustrated by Various Hands

St Edmund Hall

Saint Edmund of Abingdon, after whom the Hall is named, lived in the parish of St Peter-in-the-East when he was lecturing in the arts at Oxford (c. 1195-1200). We know that he used his lecture fees and other funds to build a chapel in honour of the Blessed Virgin. This is generally held to be the Lady chapel at the north-east corner of St Peter-in-the-East, not a stone's throw from the Hall. Edmund went to Paris for several years to study theology, then returned to Oxford as Doctor in Theology and lectured on the subject around 1214–22. Later, after his promotion as canon and treasurer at Salisbury, he became Oxford's first Archbishop of Canterbury in 1233 and was proclaimed its first saint in 1245. On a journey to Rome in 1240, he died in Soisy, France. His embalmed body is preserved in a casket over the high altar in the Cistercian Abbey at Pontigny.

Accounts of the Hall's history suggesting that it existed during Edmund's lifetime have been discredited. But although the first documentary evidence for its existence is dated 1317–18, the Hall can nonetheless claim to be among the oldest academic institutions in Oxford. Throughout the medieval period, it was one of the recognized lodgings or hostels which housed the great majority of undergraduates or graduates studying for degrees in the university. Each hall was governed by a principal approved by the university authorities. Official recognition of these scholarly societies ensured that they had a fairly strict educational regime, providing lectures and some individual instruction as well. According to John Kelly (Principal of St Edmund Hall, 1951–1979) each hall formed a distinct community, and several had a regional or even national ethos and identity: 'Just as it had earlier been natural for groups of students from, say, Wales or Ireland, or from Yorkshire, to share lodgings in the town, so the halls which developed from such households often retained a markedly local connection'. The second and third known Principals of St Edmund Hall (John and Robert Luc) came from Cornwall. The fourth, John de Bere, was from Devonshire. It seems likely that during their Principalships the Hall was, as John Kelly suggests, 'the resort of scholars hailing from the West Country'. Appropriate, then, that the chough should have become the Hall's symbol.

Quite how long the Hall's Cornish connection persisted will not be known until someone undertakes the necessary research. But it is heartening to think that this regional association may have left a lasting mark on the college. Nearer to our own times, for instance, the Cornish poet and critic Geoffrey Grigson was partly influenced by the Hall's coat of arms when the moment came for him to choose his Oxford college. He would have preferred Exeter because its gates 'had been barricaded at one time against the wrath of Jonathan Trelawny', a bishop and baronet from his own home parish, who had them broken down at his command. But Exeter was too expensive, 'and if nothing else but the Hall was possible', Grigson observes wrily, 'it pleased me that the Hall's coat-of-arms contained three [sic] Cornish choughs.' (*The Crest on the Silver*, p. 89). Always fond of his birthplace, Grigson was also pleased to discover that 'a mid-nineteenth century evangelical who had been vicar of Pelynt, had taken his degree from the Hall, before settling into Cornish obscurity and the breeding of six clerical daughters none of whom had ever married' (op. cit., p. 89). Here as elsewhere his prose has an ironic edge; but the anecdote is revealing. Regional loyalties still clearly played a part in the composition of Oxford colleges during the 1920's. Exeter was the prime college for West country people (just as Jesus was for the Welsh); but the choughs of St Edmund Hall had a symbolic pulling-power for applicants who felt a strong sense of Cornish identity.

More fancifully, one might even claim a kind of analogy between St Edmund Hall's history and that of the chough. We have preserved 'Hall' in our name out of a sense of pride in our medieval origins. Nonetheless a gradual process of tactical negotiation has been involved in our achieving the fully autonomous status of a college. Although being the only surviving medieval hall in Oxford had its charms, the Hall needed to govern its own destiny; and this was not possible once The Queen's college (our nearest neighbour) had taken over the ownership and governance of the Hall in 1557. Eventually, though, in the years between 1952 and 1957, the constitution of the Hall was revised so as to give it full collegiate status. (It is still customary at Hall events to boo when the name of Queen's is mentioned in Principalian speeches. Fortunately, though, relations between the two colleges are friendly. It is fitting that we have two poems from David Constantine, Fellow of Queen's, in this volume).

As we saw in Part Two, the chough has been associated through history with the Cornish struggle for home-rule, and with a courageous spirit that survives adversity. Recently we have been reminded of yet another layer in the bird's evolving cultural identity which links it with St Edmund Hall. In the Daily Telegraph (14 April 2001) an article appeared under the headline 'Canterbury ready to welcome back friend of Becket'. At a wildlife park just outside Canterbury, conservationists are making efforts to re-establish the Cornish chough in the countryside of Kent. The bird has special historical associations with Canterbury since, as David Sapsted pointed out in his Telegraph article, 'When Henry VIIIth ordered the dissolution of the monasteries, and decreed that no reference to the Church should appear on new coats of arms, the city submitted a new design for royal approval. It bore, as it still does, three choughs, replicating the trio on the coat of arms awarded to Thomas Becket after his assassination in Canterbury Cathedral.' Referred to punningly by conservationist David Gow as 'a subtle way of hoodwinking the crown', Canterbury's arms declared its ongoing allegiance to the Church, its defiance of Henry VIIIth, and its pride in its martyred saint.

When St Edmund's arms were invented by Archbishop Parker for his Compendium of Archbishops, he based them on the arms at Abingdon Abbey near where St Edmund was born. But a reference to Canterbury must also have been intended, given that St Edmund was one of Parker's most illustrious predecessors. Appropriately, then, our cross and choughs mingle allusions to three of our most significant historical connections, if they refer to Cornwall (associated with our early Principals); to Abingdon, birthplace of Edmund; and also to Canterbury, the destination of Oxford's famous archbishop and saint. The longstanding connection between Teddy Hall and Canterbury is also preserved in the name that was given to the new building at the far right-hand corner of the front quad in 1934. Blessed by the Archbishop of Canterbury on 10 October its opening coincided with the 700th anniversary of the consecration of Edmund of Abingdon as Archbishop.

Perhaps, in recognition of these intertwined associations, it is time that Canterbury and Cornwall clubbed together to endow a Chough Fellowship at St Edmund Hall!

Old members of St Edmund Hall are known as 'Aularians'; and in Aularian parlance, the phrase 'Hall-spirit' is used to describe the communitarian ethos and feisty independence which we share with the Chough. It has inspired the loyalty and affection of Aularians through the ages. We see it infusing the poems collected in the last section of this anthology, which have been written by Fellows and members of the Hall's staff. You have to know a little about the Hall's ethos and history to appreciate the humour that informs most of the poems in this section. Even more inside knowledge is needed to thread your way through the intricate labyrinth of Justin Gosling's 'Recently Discovered

Manuscript'. Few readers will have the expertise to decipher the medieval manuscript itself, written in dog-Latin. But Gosling's editorial notes have proved invaluable both in restoring the original context of composition, and in providing an idiomatic translation. Further knowledge of the Hall's history can be readily acquired from John Kelly's authoritative work, *St Edmund Hall: Almost Seven Hundred Years*, from which the quotations at the beginning of this introduction are taken.

L.N.

AULA Sᵀ EDMUNDI.

GORMENGHAST
CHOUGH

FLOREA TAULA

'The Slander of our Country'?

'Teddy Hall is a chough college', announced Arthur Farrand Radley. Yet some might think there were problems in associating ourselves with the famous red-legged Cornish bird. Traditionally, the word 'chough' was used in English as an insult to describe the poor and easily deluded country-dweller. Richard Brathwait's *Whimzies*, for example, first published in 1631, records a character who 'carries his trinkilo's [trinkets] about him, which makes the countrey choughs esteeme him a man of prize'. – which of course he is not. Nor did the word indicate any sympathy for scholarship: *The Return from Parnassus*, a comedy 'publiquely acted by the students of Saint Johns colledge in Cambridge' around 1600, refers to the 'thick-skin chuffes' who 'laugh at a schollers need'. Even in the later 19th century, dialect dictionaries from several countries in the south of England record that the word was then in use as an adjective to mean 'surly' and 'morose'.

Some of these attributes, no doubt, were derived from a knowledge of the bird's natural habits, for until the 19th century, the Cornish chough was common not just in the far west of England, but also in the southeast; and the name is still used by some clubs and societies in Kent. But it is especially linked with Cornwall, and has long featured in that county's heraldic devices. Cornish writers have not always welcomed the connection, though. Richard Carew's *Survey of Cornwall*, published in 1602, calls the bird the 'slander of our country': its condition 'is ungracious', he declares, 'inn filching and hiding of money and such short ends', And a few years later, when Cornwall stood out as an opponent of parliamentary sovereignty in the early stages of the Civil War, enemies of the county drew on these associations to express their hostility. The 'Cornish Chough' then became a frequent character in the pamphlet was in London – not just poor, but a pirate too.

Opponents and allies in the 17th century were all agreed on one thing, however: that the 'Choughs' were great fighters. It is also clear that all sides thought they were somehow different from the other inhabitants of the British Isles. The Cornish believed this too. The history of early-modern Cornwall is marked by a series of insurrections, in the 1490s and 1540s as well as the 1640s. The 'Cornish Choughs' thus exhibited a great sense of their own identity, and an unremitting desire to assert their autonomy.

The chough is not perhaps such an inappropriate symbol for the Hall, after all.

Nicholas Davidson

Badgered Choughs

*'Or a cross patonce gules cantoned
by four Cornish choughs'*

A person skilled in heraldry
could draw the badge
from this description.
Me? I'm too old to take up arms.
In any case the birds have flown.

More than forty years ago
I'm sure I once saw three or four
going single-mindedly about
their studies in entomology
on the front quad's smooth, forbidden lawn.
Someone said the family
lived here for centuries and used the chapel roof
to spy from, but I don't recall
ever seeing them again.

Perhaps when the Kelly building was put up
the birds went down, seeking by degrees
respite from noise and workmen.
On long vacations in Wales or Brittany
they must have found cowpats' haute cuisine
delighted them so much they didn't feel
like coming back for Eights week,
formal dinners, finals and all that
and stayed in exile, *in absentia.*

Well, let us make the most of it,
make do with specimens on cloth
or fixed in print: artificial, yes,
but in a way still very much alive–
emblazoning a great tradition.

David Clarke

The Cross and Choughs

They look a bit kinky in their red leggings, but proper, as they stride ahead, guarding four-square the precious symbol of truth and learning. Jude loved their cousins once, but that is a good omen. We hear them cawing *Aula, Aula!* down the ages, not picking over the carrion, but reassuring The Saint, Master John, and all the rest who follow them, even grouchy Hearne, that the Hall and its values endure.

Brian Gasser

'The Braggart Chough'

The Braggart Chough
A Recently Discovered Manuscript, Edited with Translation, Commentary and Bibliography by Justin Gosling.

Introduction

The following poem was recently discovered in Abingdon in a property once belonging to Abingdon Abbey. The authorship is uncertain. The combination of frivolity, ignorance and ineptitude suggest that it is a student composition, but not, one hopes, by one of the better students. The fact that it was discovered on Abbey property makes it likely that that student became a monk, or was a friend of someone who later became a monk and treasured this youthful folly(but see the note under *Bibliography*). It seems that one or both were students in Edmund's house, once situated at the northwest corner of the present front quadrangle of St Edmund Hall, Oxford. For the monk it would have served as a reminder of his happy times under the tutelage of his fellow Abingdonian, Edmund. The uncertain Latinity and regrettable lack of prosody mean that, except for the occasional touch, it is of no literary merit. Its date, however, is 1221, and this gives it considerable historical importance. First it makes it clear that the Hall existed at an earlier date than that suggested by such sceptical authorities as Emden, Kelly and Cowdrey, and at least as early as that suggested on the engraving by E.H.New (1220), and commonly believed in earlier times. It might even have been started by St Edmund himself, - he was, after all, almost certainly teaching in Oxford up to 1222. Secondly, the reference to choughs makes it clear that that association does not, as often thought, come from the vanity of a later Archbishop of Canterbury wishing to ensure that his predecessors had coats of arms, but was there, for reasons as yet unknown, from the very beginning. The original has no title.

I have appended no notes on the metre. The reckless indulgence in trochees and anapaests throws the reader, along with the author, quite off balance, and it is impossible to make the result consistent with any known form. It is not to be recommended as a model to anyone embarking on the writing of Latin verse.

In preparing this work I have been indebted to my wife, Margaret Gosling, who has generously given me the benefit of her wide knowledge both of the locality and of the historical background. Without her assistance the commentary would have been even more pathetic, in the deplorable modern sense, than it is.

J.G.

Latin Version: Untitled

"Brekekekex Corax Corax" [1]
Pueri puellae [2] *cantitant;*
Meas sic voces irrideant [3]:
"Brekekekex Corax Corax".

Scholares ebrii [4] *saltitant;*
Terga togis studii [5] *nigrant;*
Imitantur sic quos cordaces [6]
Caelestes saltant coraces.

Est mihi gloria unica
(Hanc aulares cum vident
Quantum mihi tunc invident!):
Crurum rubescens tunica. [7]

Brekekekex, corax, corax,
Nulla avis mihi est aequalis.
Nulla earum tam regalis,
Nam avium omnium sum rex, pulcherrimus, nobilissimus
                                    Cornubii Graculus Corax.

Brekekekex [8]
Kekex
Corax. [9]

English Version: The Braggart Chough

'Brekekekex Corax Corax' [1]
Chant the giddy dolls and guys.[2]
Well then, let them mock my cries.[3]
'Brekekekex Corax Corax'.

The students drunkenly cavort,[4]
With black gowns[5] on their backs disport,
Aping the airy belly dances[6]
With which the chuff its life enhances.

One glory is unique to me
(And once aularians have seen
It, with envy they go green):
The blush-red legs that you can see.[7]

Brekekekex Cherough Cherough,
Not one bird to me is equal;
None of them is half so regal;
For of all birds I am king, of surpassing beauty and nobility, the
                                    Cornish Graculus Corax, or Chuff.

Brekekekex,[8]
Kekex,
Corax.[9]

Notes and commentary

1. 'Brekekekex…' This is an adaptation of Aristophanes's *Brekekekex coax coax* in imitation of the noise of the frogs in his play of the same name. Unfortunately choughs do not sound like frogs, so this echo merely serves unhelpfully to direct the reader's mind in the direction of Aristophanic comedy. 'Corax'. Corax is a raven. A chough is not a raven. Its zoological Latin name is *Graculus Corax*. A Graculus is a jackdaw. 'Corax' may indicate student ignorance.
2. 'Pueri puellae'. Not 'boys and girls', but young men and women. It becomes clear that they are students. Given the medieval statutes for halls, some think that the text should be amended, say, to 'pueriliter'. In general, however, the harder reading should be preserved. This may throw light on an otherwise unrecorded aspect of early Hall life. Or it may be that the reference is to young women of the town.
3. This is a fine line, showing the chough's scorn: 'let them mock my cries'.
4. Hall traditions are very old.
5. 'Studii', a doubtful genitive. One might expect an adjective, but then one might not expect 'toga'. 'Their backs are black with togas of study'. Clearly what is meant is academic gowns. The *toga* was a Roman male garment sometimes adopted by loose women, and so the word is sometimes used for prostitutes. Perhaps some lewd innuendo is intended here (see note on 'puellae' above). If so, its precise nature remains obscure.
6. 'Cordax'. The cordax was a wild dance of Greek comedy. The imitation of it gave a suggestion of drunkenness and immorality. There is no evidence of choughs performing this dance. We are probably being presented with a transferred image: the students imitate this dance and the result is likened to the wheeling of choughs over the Cornish breakers.
7. 'Tunica'. This is an undergarment. The word is used poetically for the skin. 'The blushing skin of my legs' refers to the well-known feature of the Cornish chough, its red legs, which distinguish it heraldically from the legless martlet, with which it is sometimes confused by the ignorant.
8. This line is of excessive length even for the uncertain metre of the rest of the poem. Some feel that it is an anticipation of a well-known feature of the poetry of Ogden Nash. In one important respect, however, it differs from Nash: there is not a trace of humour in the line. So all it shares is crudity and immunity to elegant recitation.
9. This has been thought to be an imitation of the famous Virgilian 'pathetic half lines'. It is unlikely that that sentimental view was prevalent in the middle ages. The author more probably held the robust position that those lines merely showed the poet's, perhaps temporary, failure of imagination. The most likely interpretation here is that we have the dying fall of the smug chuckle of a self-satisfied chough, something which will be recognised by later generations. Readers are encouraged to read the poem aloud according to each interpretation and decide for themselves.

Bibliography

Not surprisingly, this work has not given rise to an extensive scholarly literature, and so has proved a boon as a research project. There is, however, one curiosity, *Corax Alazon Graculus*, by Justinus Anserculus, published at the author's own expense in the 15th. century. References in the notes to 'some who have thought…', and so on, when about the poem itself, are invariably either to this text or to beliefs I once held and have now rejected. The work itself is more notable for its pomposity than for either its accuracy or its acumen, but it is interesting evidence of the existence of another manuscript, and suggests that the work may once have had a wider readership. Perhaps a number of contemporaries formed an early society of 'Choughs' and shared their literary achievements. This suggests the possibility of a deeper, more sinister reading of the poem. At the surface level the chough is scorning the students who imitate him. At a deeper level these students can be seen as renegade members of the society (imitation 'choughs') who reject and dare to mock the one(s) who remains true to the society's traditions, the true 'chough'. The description of them as drunk may insinuate that they are legless martlets, thus underlining the fraudulence of their claims. The true chough, representative of those upholding the original principles of the society, rejects their mockery with scorn. The dispute is bitter, and divides the community. There is obviously some special significance in the possession of red legs, though what precisely that is must remain subject for speculation. The full subtlety of the symbolism and allusion is now beyond our unravelling. What *is* clear is that all was not well at the Hall at this early period. This may give hope to some aspiring scholar of a further find. Anserculus is also aware of an English translation, now lost, from which he has presumably translated the title. This is unlikely to be original, containing as it does the extremely rare transliteration from the Greek, *alazon* (although it is found in Plautus, whom our author just might have read). He presumably inserted the title for fear that some readers might fail to catch the general drift of the poem. I have translated it back for my own English version, which I venture to think, while at points a trifle free, captures well both the felicities and the crudities of the original. The work of Anserculus created not a ripple on the calm surface of contemporary or later scholarship, and I have thus been left free to present the poem fresh to the scholarly world.

It is common for scholars to say that their work has been a labour of love. This has not been so in the present case. It is difficult for those who have not endured it to imagine the tedium of labouring to pretend an interest in such worthless rubbish. I can, however, claim that no-one else has before produced a serious commentary on this work. I am, therefore, hopeful that it will boost my university's reputation for original scholarship, as it would, no doubt, had I managed to complete it before retirement, have secured my own position in the Faculty.

St. Edmund and the Chough

Aquam in manibus abbas hostibus det, pedes uero hospitibus in Christo dignis tam abbas quam cuncta congregatio lavet. Quibus lotis hunc versam dicant, "Suscepimus, Deus, misericordiam tuam in medio templi tui."

The abbot washes the hands of guests. Also, the abbot as well as the entire congregation washes the feet of the guests, worthy in Christ. After they have washed him, they say this verse, "God, we receive your mercy in the midst of your temple."
— The Rule of St. Benedict, Abingdon Copy c.1000

"Laudate Dominum de terra, drac..."
Knock! "Drat!" A knock again. "And Double Drat!"
"What now?" Edmund wondered, with a wistful
Sigh, slammed shut the Psalter. "These silly monks,"
Complained the archbishop, but with kindly care.
Meetings with monarchs, and Canterbury's
Constant conferences, clerical work
Organizing the piteous pilgrims—
Never a free moment for a gentle soul.
His sole comfort was his hairshirt. "And yet,"
He thought, "these monks are nice, mostly, without
"Cunning." And so it was with great courage
That he rose from his reading to respond to
This curious intrusion. Oaken planks
Of the door, with a brush and a scrape on the stone opened
Revealing: Nothing. "No one there. A prank."
About to shut the day light out he heard
From a creeky little throat, that seemed to croak
In language rough, a word of "Evermore."
It was a chough, a Cornish chough, who flew
On to his bishop's cross — its gloss sent forth

His reflection in all four directions—
Still saying, "Evermore." His thoughts were filled
And blest, by this image, this was the crest
Of Abingdon Abbey, ascetic seat
Of Paradise. He thought of the ebb and flow
Of long Latin, slow vowels washing against
The crevices of his mind. The crack of his knees,
Kneeling, on Good Friday, staring at worn
Sections of purple shrouds hiding, hardly,
The sorrow of our Lord. The scratch of stone
Against his fasting flesh, curtailed, yet more
Alive. Even the bite of warm small beer
In Eastertide, indulgence honoring
A guest, a mendicant, whose feet he washed,
Like a humbled God, according to the Rule.
And Edmund smiled, taking delight in days
Departed, days delicious with denial.
He broke his piece of stale black bread and shared
It with the bird, then making sure no one
Was near to overhear or to observe,
The archbishop, this regal Lord, sprinkled
Holy Water on the chough's small feet, a guest
Of Messianic worth, from days foregone.
With that, a black streak shook into the sky,
As the bird embarked westward, growing broad, long
In the shadows of the morning sun. Edmund
Was left to wonder on the wings of the chough:
And dare he dream of when his friend would come
Again?
       "...quae faciunt verbum eius."

Mike Tomko

Too Good to be True

My bird book begins its section on the chough with the words, "choughs are wonderful birds". So I have no doubt that the chough is an appropriate emblem for the Hall. But do the wonderful survive in a competitive world?

My bird book comments, "Unlike the rest of its family (the crow family), its character is as white as its plumage is black, but it has become sadly scarce." The raven is combative; the carrion crow quarrelsome; the rook truculent; the magpie cunning; the jay wary; the jackdaw a thief. The chough is vivacious, feeding the female in courtship, and fond of athletic exercise – a good Aularian – but has become scarce. In Scotland the gamekeepers shot it because of its family links. Guilt by association. Not uncommon.

Being wonderful doesn't guarantee survival. Should we note?

Ian Scargill

A Snippet of Useless Information

Ancient writers from classical times onwards have told of the belief that members of the crow family live to an immense age.

Sir Thomas Browne, the 17th century writer and "Collector of Vulgar Errors", himself an Oxford man, translated from Ansonius

"To ninety-six the life of man ascendeth
Nine times as long that of the chough extendeth".

Eight hundred and sixty four, by his reckoning. A recent list of the Arms of The Oxford colleges gives seniority to St Edmund Hall, comfortably ahead of Univ and Merton (though they may argue otherwise) with a foundation date of 1226. Taking that date we have another 89 years to run, till 2090, before mortality is likely to affect the Choughs on our crest. An encouraging thought for the Governing Body in their forward planning...

Michael Cansdale

S.E.H. in Australia

When the storm was rough
And the going was tough
It blew the poor chough
A long way down under
In a peal of thunder
Where the Ted do roam
So the Chough felt at home.

N.C. Pollock

Pourquoi aime-je les craves à bec rouge?

Pourquoi aime-je les craves à bec rouge?
Que me signifient-ils?

Quatre années heureuses,
Des cravates caractéristiques,
Des amis lointains,
Des études sans fins.

Pourquoi aime-je leurs becs du feu?
Que me signifient-ils?

La peur, la foi,
L'amour, la joie.

Je suis contente de connaître ces bêtes.
Quand même, je préfère les lapins.

* * *

Why do I like choughs?
What do they mean to me?

Four happy years,
Idiosyncratic ties,
Far away friends,
Endless studies.

Why do I like their fiery beaks?
What do they mean to me?

Fear, faith,
Love, joy.

I am chuffed to know these creatures.
All the same, I prefer rabbits.

Emma Steane

A Traditional Meal

For the feast day of St Edmund
Take some trouble with the food.
It's November: something hearty –
Roasted, casseroled, or stewed.

Though Nigella, Delia, Jamie
Show us all the fancy stuff,
All their offerings seem so samey:
Hallmen need their roasted chough.

Oven heated to two-twenty,
One per person, in the tin
With the trimmings there'll be plenty
Once the stuffing's been crammed in.

Basted ev'ry fifteen minutes
With a stock of wine and gin
Till the flesh is soft within its
Toothsome, crisp and back'ning skin.

Set aside. Now pour the juices
(And the scrapings) from the pan;
Boil fast till it reduces
To the stickiest it can.

Serve with spinach, dark and tannic,
Like a garlicked podweed stew.
(Veggies: you don't need to panic:
Peppers have been stuffed for you.)

Carried, steaming, to the table,
Served with pride, that Hallmen may
Eat as much as they are able
On St Edmund's special day.

Once a year it's what we crave. We
Bond, and gorge, throughout the hall,
Dabbing up the glist'ning gravy:
Floreat Aula, one and all.

Adrian Briggs

Λάθος

Ένα παιδί από την Αυλή
στο Άγιον Όρος είδε πουλί
μαύρο, με κόκκινα πόδια.

– Γειά σου, φίλε μου. Είσαι άγιο πουλάκι;
Εραλδικό σύμβολο
του Αγίου Εντμούντου;
Δηλαδή πυροκοράκι;

– Βρε, είσαι τυφλός ή δεν βλέπεις χρώμα;
Ο εξάδελφός μου είναι (ίσως) ιερός,
το ράμφος του κόκκινο από φωτιά και αίμα.
Εγώ, όμως, έχω ράμφος κίτρινο
από μέλι, χρυσό και ηλιοφώς·
υλικά μαγικά, αλλά όχι ιερά.
Γι' αυτό, δυστυχώς,
το αλπινό πυροκοράκι
δεν είναι σωστό για εραλδικό σύμβολο
της Αυλής του Αγίου Εντμούντου.

Χέïσελ Ροσσόττι

03/01

Mistaken Identity

A lad from the Hall
saw a bird on Mount Athos,
black with red legs.

'Hi there, my friend. Are you a sacred bird?'
The heraldic device
of St Edmund?
i.e. a chough?

Clot, are you blind, or don't you see colour?
My cousin is (perhaps) holy,
his beak red from fire and blood.
I, however, have a yellow beak
from honey, gold and sunlight,
magical stuff, but not sacred.
So, alas,
the alpine chough
isn't the right heraldic device
For the Hall of St Edmund.

Three Limericks

Alright

Birds twitter and squawk in the light;
They're hooting and screeching at night;
        They plunder your fruit;
        And crap on your suit:
But stuffed choughs in a case are alright.

Stephen Blamey

The Principal's Bird

Sharp beak, proud of manner, with plumage sleek
Come not to the Hall if it's peace you seek.
        You won't be too chuffed
        You'll find yourself stuffed
Doing time on display, like a freak.

Robert Whittaker

Lame

There was a small bird called chough
Who thought all the other birds rough,
        This limerick is lame
        Because of his name,
For which there aren't rhymes enough.

Ben Burton

Hackneyed Chough

In the winter of 1944 the British Home Service commissioned poems "about Christmas" from a number of poets, amongst them Anne Ridler and one W.H Auden. They had to be, according to the commissioning producer, as "objective as possible and to invoke the various associations of the season in the mind of the listeners". Auden submitted the "Shepherd's Carol". My own paltry imagination has been unable to establish the remotest link between this poem and Christmas beyond the reference to 'winter'. Graham Midgley however much loved it. It was sung at Auden's funeral and he asked for it to be read at his own, which it was.

I therefore submit, in the spirit, if not the style of W.H. Auden, and to the honour of my dead friend Graham the following poem about choughs.

Suburban Sunday 2000

It is lovely here
and on a quiet day
you can hear the lawnmowers.

Jeffrey Hackney

The Choughs of St Edmund Hall

I've been around, I've seen the world,
I'm a bit of a crossword buff;
But one thing I'd never heard of
Was the bird they call the chough.

They form part of the college crest
Here at St Edmund Hall
They're even seen within the quad
High up upon the wall.

Principals, bursars, tutors, students,
They'll all move on one day
But not our little feathered friends,
For they are here to stay.

Of beautiful birds around the world
There are more than enough
And so I've often wondered
Why did they choose a chough.

Life here's been like a learning curve
Like going back to school
I've learnt sayings such as 'you're a star'
And 'that's really cool'.

As time goes by and I get old
I'll forget a lot of stuff
But one thing I will remember
Is the bird that's called a chough.

David Beeching

Pedigree

See high above the rocks and cliff-face bare
Jet-black tornadoes hurtle through the sky,
To plunge and roll and twist and lift and lie
Upon the spirals of the salty air;
And as they tumble, dart and weave and pair
A loud 'Kee-yaah, Kee-yaah, Kee-yah' they cry.
Beneath their scarlet shanks the sea-stones sigh
And surge in blue-green water, clear and fair.
Upon the ragged cliffs they perch and feed
On beetles in the rabbit-nibbled grass;
They probe for insects and the farmers' seed
As countless seasons come and gently pass.
Oh, see the joyous acrobats' display
Within the theatre of a Cornish bay.

These glossy feathered cousins of the crow,
With red, curved beak and uneuphonious name,
Can put an ancient pedigree on show
To prove their worth in any hall of fame.
Great Chaucer knew their ancestor 'the thef'
Who stole upon the scene within the wood.
The Bard himself brought Gloucester in his grief
To Dover's cliff for there wise Edgar stood
And told of 'choughs that wing the midway air'.
And Holy Edmund, born in Abingdon,
Renowned for peaceful deeds and loving care,
Beloved as Oxford scholar, Oxford's son,
Shares his cross gules with four black thieves so small—
Cornubian crows to honour Edmund's hall.

Anne Adams

The Chough:
A Trip Down Memory Lane

Back in the bosky days of 1964, a group of close friends approaching graduation from the Hall were sitting round the Well one evening discussing whether and how they might stay in touch with each other after going down. In addition to the imminence of the group's separation, a further complication was that of the thirteen of them, five expected to live abroad after graduating and several others were considering short or medium term travel plans. As we struggled with the realisation than an annual weekend would almost certainly not work and even a dinner would be difficult, suddenly and with typically limpid clarity Anthony Rentoul (Jurisprudence of course) produced the solution. Starting the following January and on a twice yearly basis thereafter we would each write chronicling our thoughts and activities to a central editor who would, in turn, collate, publish and distribute the resulting newsletter. Anthony volunteered to be our first editor, to which end we all opened a Standing Order in his favour for the princely sum of £1 per annum (mine is still extant), and Peter Newell, whose family owned Wolsey Hall, the Oxford-based correspondence college, agreed to act as our publisher. All that remained was to name our little journal, and over farewell drinks in the buttery a few days later "The Chough" was born.

Initially, the Choughs were 16 in number, including three honorary members in the persons of John Kelly, Graham Midgley and Reggie Alton. We were a diverse bunch, representative of undergraduates of the Hall at that time in all respects, I would suggest, but two. First, perhaps anticipating our own diaspora, our group boasted an unusually large international element. Second, there wasn't a rugger bugger amongst us – indeed I believe I might have been the only Chough to have had the honour of representing Oxford against Cambridge, but as a mere croquet player I was barely fit to be mentioned in the same breath as the pantheon of great sporting heroes who graced the Hall in the glory days of the early 1960's.

So who were these merry men, and what became of them? David Band, a shrewd and lovely Scotsman, became a fine investment banker but tragically died of a heart attack whilst in his prime as the Chief Executive of Barclays de Zoete Wedd. Alec Georgiadis, who was our most exotic colleague, has combined his Greek charm and a swashbuckling commercial instinct to become a shipping and trading magnate. Steffen Graae came from the U.S. to read law and returned to a distinguished career culminating in his appointment to the bench in Washington. Michael Hamilton came to the Hall from Canada, stayed and has made his name in the City. Peter Newell, our original publisher, spent some time in the U.S., then ran the family business, and now looks after a range of private interests. John Parr from South Africa returned to farm in the Orange Free State where he remains to this day.

Another colonial, this time from South Africa, Nigel Pegram went on to enjoy a successful career in show business. Ian Rae, a great oarsman, joined Courtaulds and ultimately became the king of the U.K. ladies underwear market before he, too, succumbed to a heart attack long before he should have done. Anthony Rentoul pursued a career in law, banking and newspapers and is now working in the copyright field. Chuck Shirkey returned to his native U.S. to work for the Government, in particular, lecturing to the military establishment. I, Martin Smith, was initially in industry then investment banking for many years and am now as they say 'plural', my main role being to Chair the English National Opera. Mike Sproule also returned home, in his case to what we then called Ceylon, to be a family solicitor. And finally Tim, the Viscount Torrington, our only genuinely blue-blooded Chough, has been active in a range of business interests as well as occupying his seat in the House of Lords, until sadly they took it away from him.

A random basket of biographies, you might say, much like any other that could have been plucked from an Oxford College at any time over the last 50 years. Yes, but with one remarkable exception. Because of that chance intervention all those years ago by a small black bird with a red beak and matching feet, the surviving members of this little band of brothers (sadly now less the Principal – as he was always known to us – and Graham, in addition to the two mentioned earlier) do not simply remain in touch. Quite unexpectedly, this simple act of mutual communication – now, it should be confessed, a little less frequent than in the past – has been so successful in bonding us together that we continue today to be the closest of good friends. Indeed for several of us it would be unusual for even a week to go by without speaking to or seeing at least one of our Chough colleagues. This after the passage of some 37 years!

What more is there to say, but "Floreat Chough" – you are a bird of magic powers and amazing resilience!

Martin Smith

Chough of Ages

Now, at this moment, I survey the earth
In spirit or reality. I fly
Soaring above the Alps or, diving down
Cross Cornish coastline, quicker than a sigh.
Am I from Arthur? Who could ever see?
I live on legend. Becket's coat of arms,
Shakespearean lore and centuries of art
Delineate the blackest of my charms.
My future's haunted. Rare, prophetic bird
Yellow or red of beak, I drag the worm
Across some tainted turf in outer speace
Regarded from afar by alien form.

David Bolton

To Dr A. B. Emden, sometime Principal, after a suggestion that the birds at Abingdon might be martlets

Martlets for Aula?
A terrible howler –
Enough of this stuff
Just say 'Floreat Chough'.

Arthur Farrand Radley

PART SIX
Chough Frenzy

In the workshop

Chough Frenzy

When I was trying to think of a title for this anthology, one of my more mischievous undergraduates came up with 'Chough Frenzy'. He was looking back on a term at Teddy Hall, during which critical commentary classes had become poetry workshops. These exercises in collaborative writing were designed to help students to understand the crucial part played by editing in the production of finished poems. A typical workshop began with all its members writing down a sequence of associations in response to key words. The group pooled its resources by hearing the associations read aloud. Jointly it was decided which words to select for each person's finished poem. Every member of the group then went away and worked on their own. They returned the following week with a poem. This was in part formed by pooled images and shared processes of selection. But it was given its final shape by their own imagination.

The workshops involved first year undergraduates reading English, who were divided into groups of four. They were led by Jenny Lewis, with myself as an apprentice. We were writing collaborative haikus around the theme of the chough in the first half of term. The chough theme challenged us because of its novelty; and the haiku provided a conveniently compact form in which to begin our experiment with workshop composition. Strictly speaking, a Japanese haiku has three lines and seventeen syllables: five in the first and third lines, seven in the second. However, this form has loosened and become less strict with the passage of time. Our workshops allowed 'haiku' to be interpreted liberally, as a three-line poem enabling compression of form and feeling.

To show the importance of selection, ordering and editing, each group was asked to respond quickly to the following 'trigger words' – AIR, BLADE, CURVED, WINGS, RED, WIND, ARTHUR. When each person's response to these words was read aloud, the composite effect was rather like hearing a piece of music. The following week, while students were working on their individual haiku- poems, Jenny Lewis returned to the collaborative 'word reservoirs' (her metaphor) which had been produced in the two different workshops. She had written down the lists of words produced by each group as they were being read aloud. Originally, the words were recorded in a block, as unpunctuated prose. She broke these prose-blocks into stanzas with line-breaks chosen for visual effect. The result was two group-poems, made up of sounds and images. 'Different line breaks would have produced different meanings,' Jenny observed, and this showed 'how line breaks can be used either for clarification, or to emphasise ambiguities.' It was fascinating to hear Jenny read the two group poems aloud, and then to see and hear the collective poems out of which all the tributary poems had flowed.

The shared vocabulary and imagery in each participant's poem came from the process of pooling ideas, words, phrases and metaphors described above. But of course each writer also has a distinctive voice of their own.

Later in the term, participants in our poetry workshops had grown more confident, and turned their hands to Celtic Blessings. This genre was new to most of us: it is formulaic, and has some of the qualities of prayer. It belongs to an oral tradition, and is ideally suited to the collaborative method of composition we had been exploring. Here is a typical celtic blessing (taken from a volume edited by Caitlin Matthews) which we used as a model for our own compositions.

Blessing on setting forth

May the road rise to meet you.
May the wind always be at your back.
May the sun shine warm upon your face.
The rains fall soft upon your fields;
And, until we meet again, may
God hold you in the palm of his hand.

A local television crew came and filmed our 'Celtic Blessing' workshop. One of the crew, Sash Norris, was by chance an environmentalist, with a strong interest in rare and endangered species. She knew all about the Cornish chough. She also knew about poetry, being a writer who had already published. She played the part of a guinea-pig that afternoon, when we had to work with unusual speed to fit into the crew's busy schedule. Within the hour, we had written a collaborative blessing, with each person supplying a single line. In addition, Sasha Norris had produced a finished poem of her own. (Would that poems usually came so speedily!) The workshop began in my front-quad room, and ended in the graveyard of St Peter in the East. The sun was shining as the snow fell. In among the tombs and gravestones we read the collaborative blessing to camera. Sasha Norris then read hers.

The haikus and blessings chosen for this volume show the immense creative energy which can be generated by collaborative writing. All participants felt that the workshops sharpened their analytic skills. Ben Burton, one of the first years, comments as follows:

> Poetry classes have proved to be an exciting and valuable part of Teddy Hall's English course. The roles of tutor and student are forgotten, as all participate equally in the creative process, both in producing collective pieces and in sharing their individual work. In this way, class members have been able to discover and embrace their differences.

I would like to record my gratitude, and that of all the students involved in the term's work, to Jenny Lewis.

LN

Arthur blade wind wings curved air

High armoured towers
stone ideals to madness.
Impossible hope.

Swaying blades shining,
slicing the light; bloodless hate.
Run on green fury.

The cold blazing streams
blow freely imprisoned in
swerving from nothing.

How steady the wings
sound, flap-beating by silence,
waiting, hovering,

swift shadows shaping,
curving and calling and still
silently hoping.

Living leaves, breathing,
scorched in the gusting white blue
by the clear white light.

Harriet Hungerford

Blast away the traps

Soft breathless slay-space
Sweeps the clear ether, light-scorched,
Listlessly lolling.

Furious iron bleeds
Metallic glittering red,
Snip, sway, swish, thrust, slice.

The smooth sensual sex
Roll-glides through the arching shores
Shading the steep womb.

Sculpted sinews ebb,
Rhythm shakes, slicing tapered air;
Strong, swift pulse of flight.

Dance, swirling fluid, swerve,
stir tree, swim, blow, whistle, sway,
Play, blast away the traps.

The dippy king reigns,
Nobly thrusting vengeful blade,
Till myth lilts away.

Paul Mudie

Chough-Panther

In the city zoo
Images caught at my hair.
Me even wide, breathing skies.

Warm paws, soft blue sheen
Over ancient strong bone-cage
And Persia's ambers.

In these scorching bars
Iron oil-slicked smothering chains.
Kicking, blood-soaked jaws.

Ireland's losing chough.
Dark plains, pulsing red womb home:
I'll sleep in your mouth.

Melissa Bradshaw

Where have all the choughs gone?

Heroic red beak feeds the chattering
on life-edge
               of cliff.
Hop along little ledge
Between speech
               and silence.

Faithful in life,
Lived in lordly fame.
Nobility is humbled.

Chough travelling
Over whale-way
Blue-black, blue-black, red.

Silent blast of lightening wing beat
Disappearing into the distance,
A small black dot.

Caroline Boon

Burning

Quick light sears a bird
onto the mind-eye, burning
an odd glory.

Perhaps man and bird can again be one–
still and brilliant and caught in the sun.

Sam Chatfield

Flight

Air white diaphanous shield
Ice blade cuts clean through
Rapier slash knife thrust up.

Wing pulse kaleidoscopic
Blood bubble burst. loosed
plume edge urges sky smooth down.

Elizabeth Scott-Baumann

Haiku Circle

sky sky yes tremulous yes ascent spiral descent i close come my fade eyes until i here blue h mm museic a yes bue diaphany cannot resist take a peak arching over arching aching lost ah for while air pierced by black stretched there frantic majestic now carressing

Ben Burton

A Celtic Blessing

May you have the strength to voice your sharp red song
    Without thorn of envy
May you continue to travel through sea-crash, sea-spray far away
    To end of end of earth
And in force of flight with outspanned, salt-wings protect
    The vista of echoes.

Caroline Boon

Blessing

May the dream drift of pillow gift curve down for you,
May the wild bend scape you not.
May the sharp red song of beaky chicks for you unleash,
May the cragged cliff-crash lose you not.
May dragonfire legend shelter your distant vista,
May the celtic pelt thrust your wingbeat with lightning
May the buckling silence vest you with peace.

On the bleak ocean stairs may you be lifted in still safe cadence.

Elizabeth Scott-Baumann

To the Chough

A beautiful, rare bird on the verge of extinction in Britain

(Written in a poetry workshop with Jenny Lewis, Lucy Newlyn, and the
English First Years at St Edmund Hall, which I attended on behalf of Channel
6.)

May you scatter sleek, bright and splayed
Over the cliffs and scraggs still
May you probe unearthly in heaven
Keep away the cruel snipe of sniper
Feed your chicks,
And opening,
Voice the sharp, strange, scarlet song of your forebears.
May the force of flight, wing thrust, wing beat
Over kingdoms, yours-mine-ours, blast you
Bringing wisdom, peace.
On ocean stairs by moat and fairytale defended
The wind's cadence carries myth, tale, legend
Though you inhabit end of end of earth, land's end
Edge of rockpools, fringe of losing lost loss,
Though you peer over pier into extinction
Breathe the upcurrent air which bears you!
Roost safe and still, Oh chough,
Home again.

Sasha Norris

Blessing for the Cornish Chough

May the gift in streaming touch bind you
                    scarlet song open your voice

may you return to losing lost lost end of end of earth
                    Land's End

may you call back home again along that vista
                    echo home echo safe echo still

may the Celtic pelt thrust your wing-beat with lightening,
        the buckling silence vest you with peace.

may the shard of cruel thorn find-forage you not.

An opening, voicing your sharp red song
                    without thorn of envy –

yours mine ours the silence.

The St Edmund Hall Poetry Workshop

The Chough Crossword

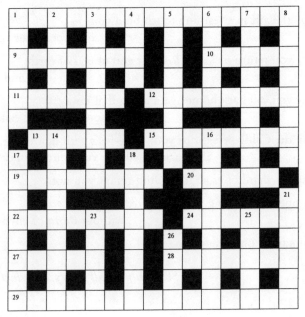

Across

1. House journal usually less explosive than it sounds. (7,8)
9. Audibly involving two sports at the back of the head. (8)
10. Scheduled amounts allowed actions around south. (5)
11. English reverend american crackers. (6)
12. Disregarding organised river going in. (8)
13. Cloth quietly put to rest. (5)
15. Uppermost section of kingdom in Antioch. (8)
19. Passive chinese female between dad and spirit gives account book. (6,2)
20. Drug rate. (5)
22. Extremely high water. (4,4)
24. First old principal, recently arrived. (6)
27. Principal german city. (5)
28. Left winger got up for Lancashire. (3,4)
29. Dull hand sent aim astray off the high. (5,6,4)

Down

1. Ouch! Ought part to fly? (6)
2. Italian girl in Scottish opera. (5)
3. Piano exit makes amends. (9)
4. Tolkien's creatures come in tens! (4)
5. A singer fellow down the river. (8)
6. Partner of visual lecturing aid. (5)
7. To start this month I restrict to College. (9)
8. Cross High tea stage hostelry. (8)
14. Fast growing trees produce line daily. (9)
16. I'm badly beaten and confiscated. (9)
17. Prepare to fire queeen; beheaded king are pets. (8)
18. Coil to guard exposed side. (8)
21. Organisation healthy? Scarcely! (6)
23. East invades lightweight cover in basic principle. (5)
25. Dame Norse god a (group of cows, 6 dn). (5)
26. Oxford has two about short road language. (4)

Nicholas Stone

List of Contributors

Contributors are listed alphabetically. An asterisk indicates that their primary affiliation is to St Edmund Hall. Other affiliations are given very briefly. Old Members are listed as Aularian. Some of the people listed have contributed notes towards the introduction, and their names are included by way of acknowledgement.

Adams, Anne	Wife of His Honour Judge John Adams, SEH Lecturer.
* Alton, R.E.	Fellow Emeritus in English; specialist in paleography; formerly editor of *The Review of English Studies*; one-time Bursar of Teddy Hall.
Bain, Iain	Aularian; Former curator of the Tate and expert on Thomas Bewick.
* Beeching, David	Head Porter.
* Blamey, Stephen	Fellow in Philosophy.
* Bolton, David	Aularian (matric. 1957).
* Boon, Caroline	JCR: reading English.
* Bourne-Taylor, Geoffrey	Bursar; Fellow; author of children's books and TV series; illustrator.
* Bradshaw, Melissa	JCR: reading English.
* Briggs, Adrian	Fellow in Law.
* Burton, Ben	JCR: reading English.
Cansdale, Hilly	Wife of Michael Cansdale
* Cansdale, Michael	Aularian; Chairman of the Old Members Association; former solicitor.
* Cardinale, Philip	Junior Dean; studying for a D.Phil in English Romanticism.
* Chatfield, Sam	JCR: reading English.
Clarke, David	Aularian (matric. 1958); poet, author of books, plays and articles; formerly headmaster of Sandbach High School.
Clarke, Gillian	Poet, broadcaster, freelance writer and lecturer. She has lived in Wales for most of her life. Carcanet have published her *Selected Poems* (1985), *Letting in the Rumour* (1989), *The King of Britain's Daughter* (1993) and *Collected Poems* (1997).
Constantine, David	Poet, translator and editor. He is an authority on Hölderlin. His most recent publication is *The Pelt of Wasps* (Bloodaxe, 2000).
Crossley-Holland, Kevin,	Aularian; FRSL; Honorary Fellow; poet, translator, editor; writer of children's books, broadcaster; most recent book, *The Seeing Stone*, shortlisted for the Whitbread prize for children's literature.
* Davidson, Nicholas	Fellow in History.
Dunn, Antony,	He won the Newdigate Prize while reading

	English at St Catherine's, Oxford. His first collection, *Pilots and Navigators*, was published by Oxford Poets in 1998 and his second, *Flying Fish*, is forthcoming from Carcanet/ Oxford Poets.
Farthing, Stephen,	Fellow Emeritus; former Master of the Ruskin School of drawing; artist.
Field, Victoria	Has lived and worked in Turkey, Russia and Pakistan and is now based in Cornwall. She is an arts consultant, and has had some of her poems published.
* Fukuda, Arihiro	Associate Professor of the History of Political Thought, The University of Tokyo.
Gasser, Brian	Aularian; Clerk to the Proctors.
Gorji, Mina	Graduate student at Lady Margaret Hall; studying for a D.Phil in English Romanticism.
* Gosling, Justin	Former Principal; Honorary Fellow.
Gosling, Margaret	Former Principal's wife.
Hackney, Jeffrey	Fellow Emeritus; Fellow in Law at Wadham.
Hollis, Matthew	Won an Eric Gregory Award in 1999, third prize in the National Poetry Competition 1996, and published a pamphlet, *The Boy on the Edge of Happiness* (Doorstep, 1996). He is co-editor (with W.N. Herbert) of *Strong Words: Modern Poets on Modern Poetry* (Bloodaxe, 2000), and currently works as an editor at the Oxford University Press.
* Hungerford, Harriet	JCR: reading English.
Jacobs, Nicolas	Poet; Fellow in English at Jesus College.
* Jenkyns, Hugh	Fellow in Geology.
Jones, Terry	Aularian (matric.1961); Honorary Fellow; writer, scholar and comedian; famed as one of the Monty Python team.
Kaspar, Susan	College Gardener; illustrator and artist.
* Lewis, Jenny	Aularian; writer of children's books; poet and teacher of creative writing in Oxford; author of *When I became an Amazon*, and recently anthologised by Carcanet.
* Martin, Priscilla	Lecturer in English; teaches Classics as well as English; writes fiction as well as criticism.
* McClure, Carol	College Secretary until her retirement in 2001.
McKendrick, Jamie	Poet in Residence at Hertford. His publications include *The Kiosk on the Brink* (OUP, 1993), *The Marble Fly* (OUP, 1997), and *The Sirocco Room* (OUP, 1991).
* Milsom, David	JCR: reading English.
* Mingos, Michael	Principal; FRS.
Mingos, Stacey	Principal's wife.
McNeillie, Andrew	Poet and Publisher (Blackwell's) His volume of poems, *Nevermore* was published by Oxford

Poets in 2000.

* Mitchell, Bruce	Fellow Emeritus in English; editor and translator; specialist in Old English.
* Mudie, Paul	JCR: reading English.
* Newlyn, Lucy	Fellow in English; specialist in English Romanticism; most recent publication *Reading, Writing and Romanticism: The Anxiety of Reception* (Oxford University Press, 2000).
Norris, Sasha	Works for Channel Six (local Oxford Television channel) Has had a number of poems published and is a keen conservationist.
O'Donoghue, Bernard	Poet, critic, Fellow in English at Wadham. He has published several collections of poetry: *The Weakness* (1991); *Gunpowder* (1995) winner of the Whitbread Award for Poetry; and *Here not Here* (Chatto, 1999).
Parker, Natalie	Aularian (matric. 1997). English and German.
Paulin, Tom	Poet, critic, broadcaster; Fellow in English at Hertford; best known for his regular appearances on BBC's *Newsnight Review*; Author of *The Day-Star of Liberty: William Hazlitt's Radical Style* (Faber, 1998) and numerous other critical works. Most recent anthology of poems: *The Wind-Dog* (Faber, 1999).
Perry, Seamus	Lecturer in English, S.E.H, 1993-5; Reader in English at Glasgow University; specialist in Romanticism; author of *Coleridge and the Uses of Division* (Oxford University Press, 1999).
* Phillips, David	Fellow and Professor of Comparative Education.
* Pollock, Norman	Fellow Emeritus in Geography.
Poster, Jem	University Lecturer in Literature with the Oxford University Department for Continuing Education and a Fellow of Kellogg College. He has been a prizewinner in a number of major poetry competitions and his first book-length collection, *Brought to Light* came out with Bloodaxe in July 2001.
* Radley, Arthur Farrand	Aularian (matric. 1935); Secretary Emeritus, S.E.H. Association.
Rawnsley, H.D.	(1850-1920). Canon Rawnsley published books on the Lake District, Wordsworth and Tennyson as well as his own anthologies of poems.
Reynolds, Susan	Lives and teaches in Oxford; works as an abstractor in various languages for Clio Press; translates and publishes poetry.
* Ridler, Anne, O.B.E	Poet and editor; formerly secretary to T.S.Eliot; anthologised by Faber.
Rossotti, Hazel,	Wife of Francis Rossotti (Emeritus Fellow of the Hall); Senior Research Fellow and former chemistry tutor at St Anne's; currently working

	on books of popular science, late eighteenth and early nineteenth centuries.
* Scargill, Ian	Fellow Emeritus in Geography; former vice-Principal; conservationist.
* Stafford, Fiona	Fellow in English at Somerville; specialist in eighteenth century and Romantic literature. Well-known for her work on Ossian, and for her book, *The Last of the Race :The Growth of A Myth from Milton to Darwin.* Most recent publication: *Starting Lines in Scottish, Irish and English Poetry* (Oxford University Press, 2001).
* Scott-Baumann, Elizabeth	JCR: reading English.
Smith, Martin	Aularian (matric 1961); banker; St Edmund Hall Fellow.
* Stafford, James	Aularian (matric. 1998): English.
* Steane, Emma	Aularian; Principal's P.A. until summer 2001.
* Stone, Nicholas	Fellow in Physics.
Tomko, Mike	Aularian; studied for an M.Phil in Romanticism; now working towards a doctorate in the States.
Trotman, John	Aularian (matric. 1972). Headmaster of The Bishop Stortford's School.
Tweddle, Mike	Reading English at Wadham.
Tweddle, Judy	Lives in Birmingham, and runs a poetry workshop for people with long-term mental health problems. Some her poetry for children is shortly to be published in *Elephants don't jump* (Belitha Press), *An Alien Stole my Underpants* (Macmillan), and *The School Year* (Macmillan).
Vance, Sylvia,	Formerly lecturer in English at SEH; now in charge of the Year Abroad programme at St Hilda's. Expert on Virginia Woolf.
Ward, John Powell	Poet and critic; has published books on Wordsworth and R.S. Thomas, as well as anthologies of his own poems.
Warner, Rex	(1905-86). Poet, novelist, translator; friend of Auden and Day-Lewis.
* Whittaker, Robert J.	Fellow in Geography; Reader in biogeography.
* Wells, Christopher	Fellow in German.
* Lucy Wilkinson	Aularian; Teaches English; illustrator of this volume.
* Williams, Bill	Fellow Emeritus in Physics.
* Williams, Patrick	JCR: reading Fine Art.
Woodd, Marcus	Artist and Lecturer in English at the University of Sussex.